Critical Thinking for Marketers

Critical Thinking for Marketers

Learn How to Think, Not What to Think

Volume I

David Dwight, Terry Grapentine, and
David Soorholtz

BUSINESS EXPERT PRESS

Critical Thinking for Marketers: Learn How to Think, Not What to Think,
Volume I

First published in 2017 by
Business Expert Press, LLC
222 East 46th Street, New York, NY 10017
www.businessexpertpress.com

ISBN-13: 978-1-63157-116-9 (paperback)
ISBN-13: 978-1-63157-117-6 (e-book)

Business Expert Press Marketing Strategy Collection

Collection ISSN: 2150-9654 (print)
Collection ISSN: 2150-9662 (electronic)

Cover and interior design by Exeter Premedia Services Private Ltd.,
Chennai, India

First edition: 2017

10 9 8 7 6 5 4 3 2 1

Printed in the United States of America.

This book's vignettes are drawn, in part, from the authors' business experiences over a collective period of 105 years, during which time the authors flew a combined 6 million miles and spent over 10 years away from home. At times we left sick kids and other domestic responsibilities in the loving care of our life-long partners. Consequently, this book is dedicated to our wives:

Cindy Dwight, Jean Grapentine, and Shelly Soorholtz

Thank you for putting up with us and always welcoming us home.

Abstract

Most marketers acquire the knowledge and skills of their trade by taking marketing and related courses in college followed by real-world experiences in a marketing career. Additionally, some read popular marketing books and attend marketing conferences. The primary thrust of this formal, on-the-job training and continuing education is to learn *what to think*. *"What are the Four P's of marketing?" "What are the steps successful sales people follow to make the sale?" "What does the customer want and need?"* A quick search on Google using the key words "what marketers need to know" turned up 32.7 million references.

All marketing actions, whether preceded by formal or informal decision making processes, are based on what philosophers call "arguments." An *argument* is a set of related statements comprising premises and a conclusion. Ideally, premises give an audience good reasons for accepting your argument's conclusion. In marketing, these "conclusions" are normative decisions about what an organization should do, for example, raise prices by 5 percent, add a new sales territory or, perhaps, change the marketing communications mix to invest more in digital and less in print. The premises are the rationale behind why the organization should take such actions.

In conducting research prior to writing this book, the authors found many good critical thinking resources in the form of books, articles, and online critical thinking courses. They found a scarcity of resources, however, specifically created to help marketers improve their critical thinking marketing skills. In short, there is a wealth of marketing resources available to tell you *what to think*, but few that help marketers learn *how to think*.

Critical Thinking for Marketers: Learn How to Think, Not What to Think provides information and guidelines on not only how to develop good arguments, but also what it means to develop a good argument. For example, the book describes two basic kinds of arguments—deductive and inductive—and how to examine whether such arguments are "good" or not. To do this, the book explains 60 logical fallacies—or errors in reasoning—that marketers should avoid. Additionally, the authors' several "Think Better" discussions that examine how fields such as philosophy, behavioral economics, and marketing theory have informed the principles of critical thinking in marketing.

Keywords

critical thinking, fallacies, logic, logical fallacy, marketing, marketing research, thinking clearly

Contents

Acknowledgments

Dr. Naresh K. Malhotra—Senior Fellow, Georgia Tech Center for International Business Education and Research; Regents' Professor Emeritus, Georgia Institute of Technology (Georgia Tech); and Editor, Review of Marketing Research—is responsible for encouraging us to research and ultimately write this book on critical thinking for marketers. His feedback and direction during the course of preparing the manuscript is greatly appreciated.

The following people provided valuable feedback and recommendations on previous drafts of this document: Kevin Gray, Cannon Gray LLC; Jean Grapentine; and, Terry Grapentine's long-time editor and friend, Lynn Coleman.

Kevin deLaplante, PhD, Founder and Lead Instructor, Critical Thinker Academy (http://kevindelaplante.com) graciously gave us permission to reprint selected sections from his Critical Thinker Academy website. Terry first met Kevin when he was an associate professor of philosophy at Iowa State University, Ames, where Terry and Kevin would occasionally discuss the philosophy of science, physics, critical thinking, and marketing, over drinks.

David Dwight
Terry Grapentine
David Soorholtz
July 2016

SECTION I

Basic Concepts

CHAPTER 1

Overview

There's a mighty big difference between good, sound reasons and reasons that sound good.

—Burton Hillis

Our Prescriptive Thesis

Bad decisions lead to marketing failures. And marketers deficient in critical thinking skills often make bad decisions. The purpose of our book is to improve your critical thinking skills so you make good marketing decisions.

We do this by first giving examples of poor ways of thinking—called logical fallacies—in a series of marketing vignettes. Then we describe how to recognize, avoid, and circumvent logical fallacies in your organizations. Additionally, we introduce you to a variety of topics related to critical thinking such as viewing marketing as a science, how cognitive biases affect judgment, and how all marketing strategies are constrained by marketing "laws."

Why We Wrote This Book

Our combined 105 years of marketing experience reveal that new product introductions are no more successful today than they were 40 years ago. In fact, many of the companies we grew up with—Pontiac, Lionel, RCA, Compaq, Pan Am, and General Foods—no longer exist, primarily due to marketing missteps over decades.

As many as 95 percent of new product introductions fail, according to AcuPoll, a Cincinnati-based research firm.[1] Do you remember New Coke, Coors Rocky Mountain Spring Water, Kellogg's Breakfast Mates, McDonald's Arch Deluxe, and HP's TouchPad? Several have become

Harvard Business Review cases demonstrating various flaws in thinking critically about new product development.[2]

Yet, during this same period, we've seen an ever-growing number of marketing conferences, seminars, and books dispensing advice to marketers on "how to be successful." A recent Google search of "marketing success" turned up 174 million references! More than ever before, a greater number of MBAs occupy the C-suite; companies spend more on marketing research; and, business "self-help" books land on *The New York Times*' best seller lists. Yet, most new product introductions fail.

How do you explain this paradox? We believe that most of these efforts to improve business performance have failed in one fundamental way: Although many organizations and consultants provide excellent advice on *what to think* when formulating marketing strategies and tactics, they have failed to help today's marketer know *how to think* about these issues. And we are not alone in this belief.

- "If you want to succeed in 21st Century business you need to become a critical thinker," says John Baldoni in a *Harvard Business Review* blog post. "… Critical thinking [knowing how to think] has always been a prized attribute of leadership, but over the years, especially as business schools have emphasized quantitative skills over qualitative ones, critical thinking dropped by the wayside."[3]
- A recent survey conducted by *The Wall Street Journal* of nearly 480 college recruiters "named some combination of critical thinking" skills as an area that college graduates need to improve most.[4]
- John Engler, president of the Business Roundtable—an association of CEOs of leading U.S. companies—says that, "In a global economy, companies will be attracted to countries where students demonstrate the knowledge [and] critical thinking abilities … to succeed at work."[5]
- Forbes' contributor Holly Green states that the number one characteristic of strategic leaders is their critical thinking skills—"the mental process of objectively analyzing a situation by gathering information from all possible sources, and then

evaluating both the tangible and intangible aspects, as well as the implications of any course of action."[6]

To improve marketing success, marketers should strive to improve their critical thinking skills. But what do we mean by "critical thinking" and how do we go about improving it?

Critical Thinking and Marketing

Marketing's central task and responsibility is making recommendations to senior management about the creation and management of the firm's marketing mix—what we have all learned as the "Four Ps":

- **P**roduct: What products should we create?
- **P**rice: At what prices should we sell our products?
- **P**lace: What channels of distribution should we use to reach our customers?
- **P**romotion: How do we communicate to our customers?

In our experience, the strength of recommendations supporting the Four Ps often dictates a marketing plan's success or failure. Sharpening one's critical thinking skills, therefore, can help you develop stronger and more successful recommendations for your organization.

So, what is "critical thinking?" One expert in the field, Edward M. Glaser, wrote the following in 1941:

The ability to think critically ... involves three things: (1) an attitude of being disposed to consider in a thoughtful way the problems and subjects that come within the range of one's experiences, (2) knowledge of the methods of logical inquiry and reasoning, and (3) some skill in applying those methods. Critical thinking calls for a persistent effort to examine any belief or supposed form of knowledge in the light of the evidence that supports it and the further conclusions to which it tends. It also generally requires ability to recognize problems, to find workable means for meeting those problems, to gather and marshal pertinent information, to recognize unstated assumptions and values, to comprehend and use language with accuracy, clarity, and discrimination, to interpret data, to appraise evidence and evaluate arguments, to recognize the existence (or non-existence) of logical relationships between propositions, to draw warranted conclusions and generalizations, to put to test the conclusions and generalizations at which one arrives, to reconstruct one's patterns of beliefs on the basis of wider experience, and to render accurate judgments about specific things and qualities in everyday life.[7]

Clearly, Glaser's definition covers a lot of ground. *Learn How to Think, Not What to Think* focuses on Glaser's second and third points, by gleaning some of the methods of logical inquiry and reasoning and applying these methods in the real world—specifically, the world of marketing.

The following vignette portrays a hypothetical recommendation proposed by John Black, vice-president of marketing for Acme, Inc., to William Smith, the firm's chief financial officer. Acme manufactures and markets anvils. The firm is going through its yearly budget review and John's team is recommending a five percent increase in the advertising budget (promotion). The rationale John gives is typical; perhaps you have heard a similar dialogue in your workplace.

William: *John, I've reviewed your marketing budget for the upcoming fiscal year and I see that your line items really haven't changed all that much from previous years. You still plan to spend the majority of your budget on television advertising and social media, with a minority of your budget going to the standard trade-shows we attend and the selected charity events we support.*

What I found a little bit surprising, John, is that you're asking for a five percent increase in your budget overall, with most of the increase going to television advertising and social media. The most I recall ever increasing the advertising budget is two or maybe three percent. I know sales are up, but, honestly, I was expecting maybe a two to three percent increase. The market isn't going to stay strong forever as much as we'd like it to. How did you come up with the five percent figure?

John: *I see where you're coming from, Bill. But our marketing team has done its homework, and we believe that we've got some good reasons to ask for that extra few percent.*

First, as you know, the company has already exceeded its aggressive sales and profit targets for this fiscal year [calendar year 2015] *and we believe that that was in large part due to last year's increased advertising budget and the new corporate image campaign we launched back in May of 2014. Most of the campaign's expenditures went into television and social media. Heck, if the advertising is working, then our sales and profits should go up. And they did. Advertising works!*

Second—and, Bill, you know this is the case, since you've been with the company for over 10 years—every year, year in and year out, marketing is always having to fight engineering, manufacturing, and customer service for every dollar in our budget. And you know what? Nothing, not even the research we've conducted, has ever shown that our advertising isn't working. That's just a fact, Bill, and that can't be ignored.

Finally, and you know this from last week's meeting, not only our advertising agency but that article I showed you from Advertising Age *has shown that companies all over the U.S. are increasing their advertising budgets— and that includes our competitors. We have to match their ad spends or our message is going to be drowned out by those of our competitors.*

I know that the five percent is high, but my team strongly believes we have good reasons for requesting that increase.

William: *I understand what you're saying, John, and it sounds to me like you're making a good case for your budget. I'll give it my preliminary approval and next week I'll recommend to the board that you get your five percent.*

Ostensibly, the marketing team's reasons for requesting a budget increase appear to be "logical." The unexpected increase in company sales and profits were indeed preceded by marketing's new advertising campaign. No one had ever offered evidence that the firm's advertising was not working and, by all accounts, competitors had indeed been increasing their advertising budgets. So William's recommendation to the board seems completely "logical."

Except that it isn't!

Marketing "Arguments"

John's rationale for requesting a five percent increase in his marketing budget takes the form of an "argument." In this context, arguments are not heated disputes between individuals yelling back and forth at each other. Rather, an *argument* is a set of statements comprising premises and a conclusion.

A *statement* is a proposition that can be either true or false. In reality, it is difficult for some marketing statements to be completely true. For example, many marketing research studies contain statistics that purport to describe markets. But these statistics are only estimates of market characteristics, and they often contain measurement and sampling errors. Consequently, statements in a marketing argument—if they can't be true with a capital 'T'—at least need to be plausible and reflect justified beliefs about market characteristics.

The *premises* are the reasons given to believe a conclusion. The *conclusion* is what you are trying to make your audience believe. "In other words, an argument tries to make you believe something, and gives you reasons to believe it."[8]

A graphical standardization of John's marketing argument is given in Figure 1.1. One way to interpret this figure is to read it from the bottom-up and insert the word "therefore" where you see an arrow. For example:

- "Sales and profits increased after increasing *this* year's budget and launching the new advertising campaign."
- *Therefore*, "Our advertising worked *this* year."
- *Therefore*, "Increasing advertising will increase sales and profits *next* fiscal year."
- *Therefore*, "We need to increase our advertising budget by five percent."

Conversely, you can read from the top-down and insert the word "because" for each arrow.

Note that John does not give William a reason for why the marketing team recommends a five percent increase in the advertising budget versus, say, a 4 or 10 percent increase. Additionally, John implies the ad budget increase and new campaign together caused the increase in company sales and profits. It's possible that the jump in sales and profits came solely from the new campaign independent of the budget increase.

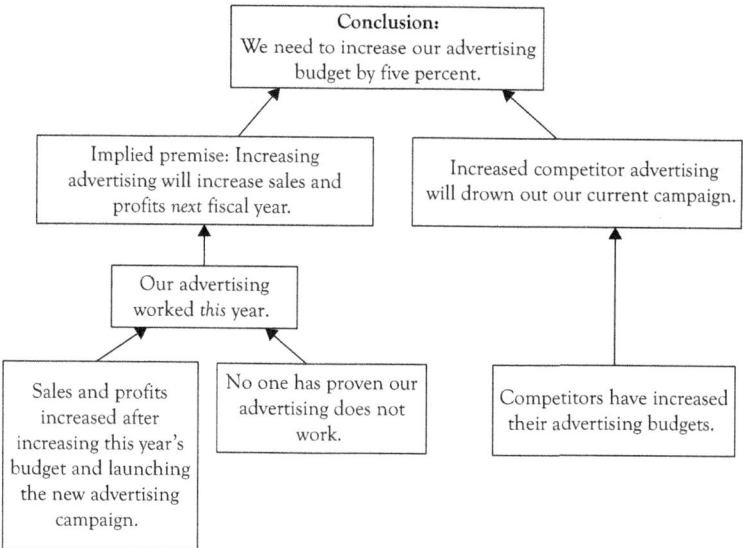

Figure 1.1 An outline of John's argument

Yet when John does give reasons to support his conclusion, none of the reasons he offers are good ones—that is, based on facts or empirically justified beliefs. For example, John uses a false implied premise to suggest that what happened this fiscal year—increased advertising supposedly led to an increase in sales and profits—will happen next fiscal year. He also states that, "Our advertising works" because "No one has proven that our advertising does not work." *In fact, all the reasons John gave to William to support the ad budget increase are described as logical fallacies.*

Logical Fallacies

If you search the term *logical fallacies* on the Internet, your search engine will produce over a million references, many with slightly different and perhaps confusing definitions of this term. Often, the terms *fallacy* and *logical fallacy* are used interchangeably, plus there are many different types of fallacies.

Consider a *fallacy* as an argument that uses bad reasoning—the kind of reasoning John used to convince William to increase the advertising budget. Examples of bad reasoning are using false, irrelevant, or weakly supported propositions to support an argument, or poor logic connecting the premises of an argument to the argument's conclusion. The Internet Encyclopedia of Philosophy elaborates on the nature of fallacies:

> Fallacies should not be persuasive, but they often are. Fallacies may be created unintentionally, or they may be created intentionally in order to deceive other people. The vast majority of the commonly identified fallacies involve arguments, although some involve explanations, or definitions, or other products of reasoning. Sometimes the term "fallacy" is used even more broadly to indicate any false belief or cause of a false belief.[9]

In the earlier sketch, John did not intentionally use fallacies to deceive William, although William unwittingly accepted John's reasons. Let's look more closely at the fallacies that John used:

- *Heck, if the advertising is working, then our sales should go up—and they did!* This fallacy is called Affirming the Consequent. We will explain later the origin of this term and the other names by which it is known. For now, consider the following relationships:

• If P is true, then Q is true.	→ If our advertising is working (P), then our sales and profits will increase (Q).
• Q is true.	→ Sales and profits increased (Q).
• Therefore, P is true.	→ Therefore, it's true that our advertising is working (P).

In this argument, the truth of Q does not logically guarantee the truth of P. Q could be true because of factors other than P. For example, an increase in sales and profits could be caused by a growing economy, mistakes made by competitors, or an improvement or expansion of the company's channels of distribution. In the extreme case, the increase in sales and profits may not have been affected by the advertising at all.

- *Advertising caused sales to increase this year; advertising will cause sales to increase next year:* Even if you grant John his premise that the recent image campaign did cause sales and profits to increase this year, that fact does not *by itself* strongly support the contention that advertising will cause sales to increase next year. Evidence supporting John's claim, however, could come from a marketing research study showing, for example, how the company's advertising increased top-of-mind brand awareness, which positively changed brand attitudes, which increased brand purchase intentions, and eventually caused sales to increase. John's unsupported assertion, however, does not give good reasons to believe that the same events will occur next year.

- *Nothing, not even the research we've conducted, has ever shown that our advertising isn't working.* This is the Arguing from Ignorance Fallacy. Just because no one has proven a given proposition false *is not* a good reason to assert that that proposition is true.

- *We have to match our competitors' ad spends or our message is going to be drowned out by theirs.* Appeal to Popularity is often invoked to support a proposition based on the following reasoning: If everyone else is doing "X," we should be doing "X," too. The fact that one's competitors have increased their advertising is not evidence that increasing one's own advertising will protect or lead to increased company sales, market share, and profits. All other factors held constant, increased competitor advertising could actually increase Acme's sales, share, and profits by increasing consumers' general awareness of the product category. This famously happened to Apple's computer line in 1981–1982 when IBM introduced its first PC. IBM's new product validated, in a sense, the new product category that Apple pioneered and led to increased sales of the Apple II.[10]

Fallacies sometimes creep into our arguments unconsciously. For example, how often have we marketers used the Ad hominem (i.e., attacking the person) fallacy—"they don't know anything about marketing"—to discount the sales department's advice about advertising or promotion programs? How often has an advertising agency used the Ambiguity fallacy when recommending that a company promote a particular product feature because that feature is "important" to consumers? The term *important* has multiple vernacular meanings. It can refer to a product attribute that consumers desire *and* affects their brand choice. Or it can refer to an attribute that consumers desire but does not affect brand choice (e.g., everyone values driver-side air bags but, since all vehicles must have them by law, they do not affect brand choice).

Since you are reading this book, we can safely assume that you will not use fallacies to support your marketing recommendations. But what of your colleagues? What happens when you are confronted with a marketing recommendation that is propped up on a fragile foundation of fallacies?

Dealing with Fallacies

Everyday business-world interactions often require marketers to respond to recommendations riddled with fallacies. The people who make these recommendations are sometimes difficult to deal with or irrational. One of them might even be your boss. What can you do in these situations?

This book contains 60 fallacy vignettes giving you advice on how to identify, understand, and deal with different fallacies when you encounter them. We did not invent these fallacies; we are simply looking at them through a marketing lens in order to help other marketers avoid some of the mistakes we have seen (and made) in our careers.

Each fallacy can be found in the existing literature. Many have cool Latin names, which gives you an idea how long fallacies have been around.

For example, consider the Alleged Certainty fallacy. Alleged Certainty is a claim that presupposes its own truth (e.g., "*Everyone knows* that attending industry conventions leads to better distributor relationships;" "*We all know* that quality sells"). Some recommendations for dealing with Alleged Certainty are as follows:

1. Although it is second nature to try to assess the speaker's intentions, don't. The logical "high ground" is to treat the Alleged Certainty fallacy as an honest attempt to state what the speaker feels should be obvious to all.

2. If the fallacy is innocuous (has no bearing on the business), let it go.

3. If it will potentially affect the business, ask the speaker for supporting facts in a nonthreatening way. For example:

"That sounds logical to me; what's that based on?"
"That's a really interesting point—was anyone else aware of that?"
"That may well be the case, but do we have the data to support that?"

More generally, when others use poor reasoning in an attempt to convince us of a marketing recommendation, try to "show how their arguments and beliefs are inconsistent with other beliefs they hold."[11] For example:

Bill (Director of Sales): *I like the new product features that R&D came up with at their off-site brainstorming meeting and I think we should incorporate all of them into our entry-level lawnmower. In fact, the more features we can put on our entry-level line, the better, assuming of course we're still price competitive. Our retail partners will love it!*

Frank (VP of Marketing): *Well, we certainly want to keep our retailers happy. But tell me Bill, is it really true that the more features we put on the entry-level mower, the better? When we did our research, what mower feature did entry-level buyers most value?*

Bill: *Let me think, oh, yes, the entry-level buyer wanted simplicity and not a lot of extra features that can make the mower too complicated to operate or maintain. I see your point. We should save those extra features for our mid- and upper-level mowers where the target customer likes a lot of bells-and-whistles.*

Based on research the company had conducted, Bill was guilty of assuming that adding additional features to an entry-level lawnmower makes it more attractive to the target customer. Frank's questions revealed to Bill that he *holds contrary beliefs*. Bill's belief that (a) target consumers will value added features on an entry-level lawnmower is inconsistent with his belief that (b) target consumers want a simple, easy-to-operate and maintain lawnmower.

Marketing Theory and Logical Fallacies

As used in this book (as well as any book on science or social-science), a theory is an explanation that possesses some empirical support. Theories, in varying degrees, help us explain, understand, predict, and often control aspects of the world.

Clearly, some theories are more developed and tested than others. The theory of evolution (first noted in Alfred Russell Wallace's correspondence with Charles Darwin on evolution by natural selection in 1858 and Darwin's 1859 *The Origin of Species*) has existed longer and has more empirical support than, say, the theories supporting dark matter (established by Vera Rubin in the late 1970s of the Department of Terrestrial Magnetism at the Carnegie Institution of Washington) and dark energy (developed in 1988 by two teams of astronomers led by Adam Riess of John Hopkins University and Saul Perlmutter of the University of California, Berkeley).

Marketing has its theories, too. Perhaps the most well-known is the theory of supply and demand, originating from the field of economics, and salient in all marketers' minds when it comes to pricing a product (i.e., the third P in marketing's Four Ps).

Marketers whose knowledge of marketing theories is deficient are more prone to using logical fallacies to support an argument. For example, consider the following case, in which Marketer #1 is proposing to be the first competitor in a market to create a customer loyalty program, and Marketer #2 is making a counter argument not to do so.

The point of this example is not to prove that loyalty programs are ineffective. Rather, the point is to show that Marketer #1's argument does not give factual or otherwise good reasons to support his conclusion, which are based on several logical fallacies.

Almost certainly *everyone* does not agree that these programs work (Alleged Certainty). Just because loyalty programs are popular with major retailers, does not mean that they will work for Marketer #1's company (Appeal to Popularity). Finally, the conference speaker's background is unknown (Appeal to Authority).

In contrast, Marketer #2 bases his conclusion on marketing studies and peer reviewed research conducted by an internationally acclaimed

Marketer #1		Marketer #2	
Statements	**Logical fallacy**	**Statements**	**Basis**
Everyone knows that customer loyalty programs work.	Alleged Certainty	None of our competitors currently have customer loyalty programs so there is no pressure for us to adopt one.	Secondary research of competitor activities
All the major retailers have these programs.	Appeal to Popularity	Loyalty programs generally don't work because they give unnecessary incentives to customers who already buy from us.	Appeal to Authority based on extensive research conducted by the
I was at a conference where one of the speakers talked about the success of these programs.	Appeal to Authority*	Loyalty programs don't work because they rarely attract heavy buyers who shop our competitors.	Ehrenberg-Bass Institute for Marketing Science, University of South Australia[12]
Therefore, we *should* start a customer loyalty program.		Therefore, we *should not* start a customer loyalty program.	

Note: *Appeal to Authority is a logical fallacy if the authority is not strongly justified. For Marketer #1 it isn't; for Marketer #2, it is.

market research institute. In the following chapters, we will draw several more examples from the Ehrenberg-Bass Institute for Marketing Science to help you think more critically in developing marketing arguments and avoid logical fallacies.

Similar examples of how marketing theory and other "thinking tips" can be used to inform sound marketing arguments will appear in a separate section of the book under the title "Think Better." Here's the first one.

Background Knowledge

Background knowledge is the sum total of all our knowledge and experiences. It informs our view of the world and the quality of the decisions we make as marketers.

Through a broad base of knowledge and experiences, we hope to make more successful recommendations to the organizations we serve. However, there's a catch ... a dirty little secret of strengthening one's critical thinking skills that is often overlooked in critical thinking books. As articulated by Kevin deLaplante, PhD, Founder and Lead Instructor, Critical Thinker Academy (http://kevindelaplante.com):

> ... The dirty secret of critical thinking instruction, which everyone knows if they've done it for a while, is that while logic and argument analysis are necessary components of effective critical thinking, they aren't sufficient, not by a long shot. What's missing is the importance of background knowledge.
>
> Background knowledge informs critical thinking at multiple levels, and in my view it's among the most important components of critical thinking. But you can't teach background knowledge in a one-semester critical thinking course—or, at least, you're very limited in what you can teach. That's the dirty secret that most textbooks avoid talking about. The most important component of critical thinking can't be taught—at least, not in the way you can teach, say, formal logic and fallacies.

Background knowledge comes from learning and living in the world and paying attention to what's going on. Mastering this component of critical thinking requires a dedication to life-long learning, a genuine openness to different points of view, and a certain humility in the face of all that you don't know. This isn't a set of skills you can master with worksheets and worked examples. This is a philosophy, this is a lifestyle choice. Textbooks don't talk about this. Or at least not as much as they should.[13]

Kevin's message is critical to those of us who want to become successful marketers. This is especially true, given how much the field of marketing has been changing just over the past five years, with major developments in Internet-based channels of distribution, promotion, and social media. Moreover, other academic fields, such as behavioral economics, anthropology, psychology, Big Data, and neuroscience, are informing the latest marketing thinking.

In this light, the last chapter in this book provides a discussion and references for building your background knowledge in marketing and related fields.

Now ... let's begin learning how to think better!

Chapter Takeaways

- Bad decisions lead to marketing failures. Poor critical thinking skills increase the likelihood that bad decisions will be made.
- Marketing recommendations take the form of arguments. An argument is a set of statements comprised of premises and a conclusion.
- Logical fallacies are instances of poor reasoning in arguments. Poor reasoning results in invalid or weak arguments.
- When you are on the receiving end of a bad argument, take the high ground; don't tell the person making the argument that's she's made a mistake. In a nonthreatening way, ask for supporting facts. *"Sounds like you are making a good point; what's that based on?"*
- Background knowledge informs the marketing arguments (i.e., recommendations) you make. Greater background knowledge will give you the resources you need to make good marketing arguments.
- Building one's background knowledge is a life-long journey of intellectual inquisitiveness.
- Start your journey today!

CHAPTER 2

The Nature of Marketing Arguments

As we discussed in Chapter 1, an argument is a set of statements comprising premises and a conclusion. Because arguments are meant to persuade, some philosophers do not insist that arguments contain True, with a capital "T" premises. Rather, an argument's premises simply need to be persuasive to your audience—that is, you need to supply your audience with good reasons and logic to believe that your argument's claims are true. Here's how Professor Kevin deLaplante explains this qualification:[1]

> Let me just wrap up with an objection to this modification that [premises just need to be plausible to one's audience and not necessarily true] … Some people might object that what I've done here is redefined the concept of truth into something purely relative and subjective, that I'm denying the existence of objective truth.
>
> This isn't what I'm saying. All I'm saying is that the *persuasive* power of an argument isn't a function of the *actual* truth of its premises. It's a function of the subjective plausibility of its premises for a given audience. A premise may be genuinely, objectively true, but if no one believes it's true, then no one will accept it as a premise, and any argument that employs it is guaranteed to fail, in the sense that it won't be judged by anyone as offering good reasons to accept it.
>
> This point doesn't imply anything about the actual truth or falsity of the claims. We can say this and still say that claims or beliefs can be objectively true or false. *The point is just that the objective truth or falsity of the claims isn't the feature that plays a role in the actual success or failure of real world arguments.* It's the subjective plausibility of premises that plays a role ….

From now on, we use the term *true* to mean a premise that is either true with a capital T or plausible to your audience.

There are two general kinds of arguments—deductive and inductive. "A *deductive argument* is an *argument* that is intended by the arguer to be (deductively) *valid*, that is, to provide a *guarantee* of the truth of the conclusion provided that the argument's premises (assumptions) are true."[2] We come across deductive arguments in fields such as mathematics (e.g., geometry), physics (e.g., Newton's laws of motion), and chemistry (e.g., how various elements interact with each other). For example, given a certain amount of purified water, atmospheric pressure at 1,000 mb, a temperature of 0°C, and the laws of physics (our argument's premises), our conclusion that water will freeze *is guaranteed*.

By contrast,

> An *inductive argument* is an argument that is intended by the arguer merely to establish or increase the probability of its conclusion. In an inductive argument, the premises are intended only to be so strong that, if they were true, then it would be *unlikely* that the conclusion is false.[3]

If a firm increases its marketing and advertising budgets—the premises of a marketing strategy—the conclusion that sales will increase is likely, but not guaranteed. Nearly all good arguments in marketing are inductive (not deductive) because, if their premises are true, their conclusions are not *guaranteed* to be true—they are just likely to be true.

Figure 2.1 shows a few terms related to deductive and inductive arguments. Deductive arguments can be valid or invalid and, if they are valid, they can also be sound or unsound. A *valid argument* is one in which, if the premises are *assumed to be true*, then the conclusion is guaranteed to be true. For example, consider the following argument:

- Premise 1: If a sales rep exceeds her sales quota by 20 percent, she is eligible for a salary bonus of 10 percent.
- Premise 2: Mary exceeded her sales quota by 25 percent.
- Conclusion: Therefore, Mary is eligible for a 10 percent salary bonus.

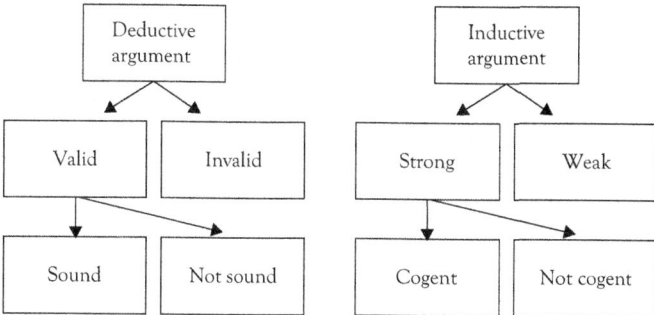

Figure 2.1 Deductive and inductive arguments

This argument is valid because if you assume that the premises are true, then the conclusion is guaranteed to be true. Furthermore, if the premises are indeed true, then the argument is sound. So all sound arguments are valid, but not all valid arguments are sound, as in the following example:

- Premise 1: All dogs are robots.
- Premise 2: Spot is a dog.
- Conclusion: Therefore, Spot is a robot.

This is a valid deductive argument because if you assume that the premises are true—even though in reality dogs are not robots—the conclusion is true. This argument, however, is not sound because one of the premises is false—all dogs are not robots.

In contrast to valid or invalid, and sound or unsound deductive arguments, inductive arguments can be strong or weak, and cogent or not cogent. A strong inductive argument is one in which, if the premises are true, then the conclusion is likely, but not guaranteed to be true. The answer to the question, "How likely does an argument need to be to be considered 'strong'?" is subjective. It depends on whether or not your audience is persuaded that your argument is likely.

If an inductive argument is strong and the premises are true, the argument is cogent. For example, consider the following simple (and admittedly incomplete) marketing argument to help explain *strength* and *cogency*:

- Premise 1: Increases in perceived brand quality, all other factors held constant, cause increases in market share, based on a recent marketing research study.
- Premise 2: Our product is perceived to possess only average quality among consumers who considered but rejected our brand, based on a recent marketing research study.
- Conclusion: Therefore, if we can improve prospects' perceptions of our brand's quality, all other factors held constant, market share will increase.

This is a strong inductive argument because, if you assume true premises, the conclusion is likely.[4] Your audience would have good reason to accept this conclusion because Premise 1 serves as a kind of "law" or empirical regularity in the market, which, when combined with Premise 2, makes the conclusion likely. (Clearly, other premises are required to make this a stronger argument—for example, high-quality brands need to be competitively priced.) The argument is cogent because (1) it is a strong argument and (2) the premises are plausible because they are based, presumably, on valid research.

Returning to a comment we made earlier that marketing arguments are nearly always inductive, not deductive. There are several reasons for this. First, marketing behavior is not deterministic as are many physical laws such as gravity. For example, although the law of supply and demand says that the quantity demanded of a product is inversely related to its price, sometimes when a product's price increases, demand increases too. Consider the following story recounted by Rand Fishkin:[5]

Savador Assael, the Pearl King, single-handedly created the market for black pearls, which were unknown in the industry before 1973. His first attempt to market the pearls was an utter failure; he didn't sell a single pearl. So he went to his friend, Harry Winston, and had Winston put them in the window of his 5th Avenue store with an outrageous price tag attached. Then he ran full page ads in glossy magazines with black pearls next to diamonds, rubies, and emeralds. Soon, black pearls were considered precious.

Second and related to the above, consumers are not robots. We assume that they have some kind of free will. No matter how compelling a marketer might believe his marketing offer is, sometimes consumers won't buy it.

Third, often the premises of marketing arguments contain information about the features of a market—how many potential consumers are in a given market, competitor market shares, information on what motivates brand choice, and so on—and this information is inaccurate or incomplete. For instance, marketing research—a great tool for measuring attributes of a market—can often only *estimate* these attributes. These characteristics generally cannot be measured with 100 percent *accuracy*—often research projects interview samples of populations and not entire populations—and small amounts of measurement error (e.g., respondents not answering questions accurately) may greatly affect the likelihood of our conclusions. Additionally, once a research study is complete, the market may have changed. In short, marketers rarely possess perfect knowledge; consequently, marketers' arguments at best can be inductively strong, but rarely deductively valid.

In conclusion, instead of trying to formulate valid and sound deductive marketing arguments, strive for strong and cogent inductive ones. Certainly, one way to do this is to avoid using the logical fallacies defined in this book. Other ways are presented in subsequent Think Better sections.

Chapter Takeaways

- To make good arguments, your premises need to be at least plausible to your audience; they don't need to be true with a capital "T." For simplicity, we use the term *true* to mean a premise that is either true with a capital "T" or plausible to your audience.
- If you intend for your argument's conclusion to be guaranteed, given true premises, you are making a deductive argument. If you simply intend for your argument's conclusion to be likely to your audience, then you are making an inductive argument.
- A deductive argument is said to be *valid* if its conclusion is guaranteed, assuming true premises. A valid deductive argument is *sound* if its premises are also true.
- An inductive argument is said to be *sound* if its conclusion is likely, assuming true premises. A sound inductive argument is said to be *cogent* if its premises are also true.
- Marketing arguments are almost nearly always inductive because human behavior is not deterministic in nature and marketers do not possess perfect knowledge.
- Avoiding logical fallacies contributes to making good arguments.

CHAPTER 3

The Nature of Logical Fallacies

This book covers a total of 60 formal and informal logical fallacies. But what distinguishes a formal from an informal logical fallacy? Basically, formal fallacies are errors in reasoning where the form of the argument does not always guarantee a true conclusion, while informal fallacies are reasoning errors in an argument's content or premises. Let's unpack what these terms mean.

A formal fallacy is *not* an error of reasoning made by someone wearing a tux and black tie. Rather, it's an error of *reasoning*—intentional or unintentional—attributable to the "form" of a *deductive* argument, independent of its content. (Recall that a deductive argument is a series of premises and a conclusion where, if the premises are assumed to be true, the truth of the conclusion is guaranteed.) Consider the following:

Argument form: This form of argument is called *Modus Ponens* (Latin for "mode that affirms")	Example
• If P (is true), then Q (is true).	• If a customer purchases six bottles of our wine (P), then she is eligible to receive a 10 percent discount on the purchase price (Q).
• P (is true).	• The customer purchased six bottles of our wine (P is true).
• Therefore, Q (is true).	• Therefore, the customer is eligible to receive a 10 percent discount on the purchase price.

An argument's form refers to the argument *as a whole*—its "structure"—and examines how the argument's structure affects the argument's validity, independent of its content. In the previous example, the argument's form is called *modus ponens* and its structure is defined in the left column. The argument's content is given in the right-hand column. In this example, assuming true premises, the argument's form guarantees the truth of the conclusion.

In a *formal fallacy*, the argument's structure does not always guarantee that the argument's conclusion is true. Affirming the Consequent is an invalid argument form and all arguments in this form are invalid because even if all the premises are true, the conclusion is not guaranteed to be true. Consider the following example:

Argument form: This form of argument is called *Affirming the Consequent*	Example
• If P (is true), then Q (is true).	• If our advertising works, then sales will increase.
• Q (is true).	• Sales increased.
• Then, P (is true).	• Therefore, our advertising worked.

Regardless of the content of this argument, the conclusion is not logically guaranteed to be true. Other factors could have caused sales to increase outside of the advertising. For example, competitors could have raised their prices or had distribution problems in getting their product on retailers' shelves. Thus, sales might have increased, but not necessarily because of the firm's advertising.

In an *informal fallacy*, it is not the argument's form that is in error; rather, we are concerned about the *content* of an argument and whether the argument's content gives your audience good reasons to believe the argument. Thus, an *informal fallacy* is a statement used as a premise that is irrelevant, ambiguous, vague, or offers a poor or bad reason to accept an argument's conclusion.

Most of the logical fallacies in this book are informal fallacies because they reflect poor reasoning based on the content of an argument. For example, consider the informal fallacy *Ad hominem* (attacking the person), which we discussed in Chapter 1. It is an informal fallacy because attacking the source or the person making a claim *by itself* is not a reason to accept an argument's conclusion. If you want to diminish the credibility of a source or person in an argument, you must provide evidence that that source or person should be discredited—for example, the source or person has a conflict of interest.

In summary, logical fallacies are errors in reasoning, which are characterized as being either formal or informal in nature. Formal fallacies are errors in the form or structure of an argument, irrespective of the argument's content, such that the argument's conclusion is not guaranteed to be true. An informal fallacy refers to an argument's content, irrespective of the argument's form, which gives one's audience a poor or irrelevant reason to believe the argument's conclusion.

Eschewing formal or informal logical fallacies will give your audience good reasons to believe what you have to say. And that's no fallacy!

Chapter Takeaways

- Some arguments assume a given "form." An argument's form refers to a specific arrangement and relationship of the argument's premises and conclusion. This chapter introduced you to two argument forms: Modus Ponens and Affirming the Consequent.
  - o Some argument forms, such as Modus Ponens, guarantee the truth of the argument's conclusion, assuming true premises. These are called valid deductive arguments.
  - o Some argument forms, such as Affirming the Consequent, do not, and are called formal logical fallacies.
- The problem with an informal logical fallacy is not its form, but rather its content. An informal fallacy is a statement used as a premise that is irrelevant, ambiguous, vague, or offers a poor or bad reason to accept an argument's conclusion. In marketing, most of the fallacies you encounter will be informal versus formal fallacies.
- The next chapter will introduce you to several more formal logical fallacies that you are well advised to avoid when making marketing arguments.

Informal and Formal Logical Fallacies

CHAPTER 4

Formal Logical Fallacies in Marketing: Introduction

This chapter introduces you to six formal logical fallacies in marketing compared to the 54 informal logical fallacies discussed in Chapter 5. Since most marketers' arguments are inductive and not deductive in nature, one does not often come across formal logical fallacies in marketing. Nonetheless they do occur, and when they do, they can be subtle and lead to some disastrous outcomes if not checked.

Formal logical fallacies can be subtle for two reasons: First, they often sound valid. The statement, "Average sales for each of our sales reps increased six weeks after we initiated the new sales training program. That was a great sales training consultant we hired," sounds valid, but isn't, as you'll read in the *Affirming the Consequent* vignette later in this chapter. Second, formal logical fallacies can be difficult to identify without examining the logical connections of the premises using pencil and paper, as we demonstrate in the upcoming *Illicit Minor* logical fallacy.

Recall that a formal logical fallacy is an argument form whose structure does not always guarantee that the argument's conclusion is true. Another way of thinking about formal logical fallacies is that they are non sequiturs. *Non sequitur* means "does not follow." So in a formal logical fallacy, the conclusion does not follow—it's not guaranteed—from the argument's premises.

The six formal logical fallacies that follow are culled from dozens that you can find on the Internet and they are the ones that we have most experienced in our marketing travels.

Affirming a Disjunct

Location: Conference room at dry-cleaning franchise company.

Issue: The marketing team is debating why their franchisees' sales have been declining over the past 18 months.

> Karen (VP franchise relations): *"We are, of course, worried about our franchisees' sales because, if their sales go down, so do our profits."*

> Jack (EVP marketing): *"How do you explain this? It seems to me that either our franchisees' customer service is declining or our franchisee marketing programs are not working."*

> Karen: *"I've reviewed the most recent marketing research studies, and they do show that customer satisfaction with our franchisees' service has declined over the past 18 months."*

> Jack: *"That makes me feel a bit better, because I'd hate to think our marketing programs weren't working."*

Jack is making a number of mistakes in his reasoning. Chief among them is that, when two reasons are offered to explain declining franchise sales, and if the evidence supports one of the reasons, then the other is false.

Definition: *Affirming the Disjunct* is a formal logical fallacy that takes the following structure:

1st Premise: If P or Q.	Franchisees' customer service is declining (P) or the company's marketing programs are not working (Q).
2nd Premise: P is true.	Research supports that P is true.
Therefore, Q is false.	Therefore, the contention that our marketing programs are not working (Q) is false.

In logic, a disjunction or "disjunct" is a compound sentence formed by combining two claims (i.e., statements) using the word "or." In the previous argument, there is no *logical reason* why Q is false if P is true; thus, Jack's statement is fallacious.

Discussion: The marketing world is often grey, not black and white, but people are often more comfortable with definitive answers.

In our example, there may be other reasons explaining why franchisees' sales have been declining beyond simply poor customer service or a failed marketing program. For instance, a declining economy, more and better competitors, or changing traffic patterns and demographics in the stores' trading areas, may explain declining sales. What's more, the reasons may be difficult to express in an absolute form—the marketing program may not have failed per se, but it could be only 80 percent as effective as hoped.

Dealing with Affirming a Disjunct

Be on the lookout for arguments using the disjunct "or." When you come across one, ask the following questions:

- Are there just two or even one claim being considered to support a conclusion? In our example, Karen and Jack only identified poor customer service and a failed marketing program as potential causes of reduced store sales. Is the conclusion, if true, brought about by more factors?
- Once you've identified the relevant factors supporting a conclusion, ask the following: Is it the case that a factor's presence or nonpresence explains an outcome, or are there degrees to which a factor is present that best explains an outcome? In our case, it's likely that the marketing program did not utterly fail—some parts of it probably worked and other parts either did not work well or indeed failed. Often, factors explaining a marketing outcome are not mutually exclusive.

Answers to the previous questions should help clear away muddled thinking that leads to Affirming a Disjunct. Whenever you encounter the word "or" in an argument, your fallacy detector should go off and lead you to examine all the alternatives more closely.

Affirming the Consequent

Location: Off-site meeting between Human Resources (HR) and the sales department.

Issue: HR and sales force management are reviewing the results of a sales training system the company has had in place for 18 months.

> Tom (human resources VP): *"My department has reviewed the sales force's performance before and after we deployed the new training system. Sales are up and I, for one, would attribute that to the new training system. What do you think, Brian?"*

> Brian (sales VP): *"Well, we spent a lot of time screening different training system companies, and it seems we selected the right one. I vote that we continue with the program."*

> Tom: *"I agree, Brian."*

Tom and Brian are assuming that the improved performance of the sales force can be attributed to the training program, and their inference seems reasonable. If the sales training program is effective, and all other factors are held constant, sales would increase. Sales increased; therefore, the sales training program has been effective. This conclusion may be correct, but the logic isn't.

Definition: *Affirming the Consequent* is a type of argument that takes the following form:

- Premise: If A is true, then B is true.
- Premise: B is true.
- Conclusion: Therefore, A is true.

In the previous vignette, Tom's argument takes this form:

- Premise: (A) If the sales training system is effective, then (B) sales will increase.
- Premise: Sales increased.
- Conclusion: Therefore, the training system is effective.

However, Tom's argument is not valid. Validity in this context means that, if his argument's premises are true, his conclusion is *guaranteed* to be true. The classic example of this kind of validity, which you probably first came across in college, is demonstrated in the following argument:

- Premise: All men are mortal.
- Premise: Socrates is a man.
- Conclusion: Therefore, Socrates is mortal.

In this example, the premises are true and, as such, they logically guarantee the conclusion to be true—if Socrates is a man and all men are mortal, by definition, Socrates is mortal. In contrast, the logical structure of Tom's argument simply does not guarantee his conclusion to be true because other factors may have caused the sales increase. "If the sales training system is effective, then sales will increase" is Tom's premise but it is not a truism like "All men are mortal." Tom set it out as a true premise but that does not mean it is true. Training is not guaranteed to achieve the results; it might, it should, but it is not a certainty. Sales and training have a more complex relationship than death and taxes.

Discussion

Sales might have increased, for instance, because of an improving economy, mistakes made by competitors, changing consumer tastes, or the simple fact that the sales force is 18 months older and more experienced. Of course, you might find this to be a trivial logical fallacy or one that is self-evident. After all, we all know that "correlation is not causation." Nevertheless, training programs are expensive and management should require better justification to approve such expenditures.

Tom should be looking for multiple, empirically based indicators that support the belief that the sales training program is working. He should not just focus on the single metric of sales volume if he wants to make a strong argument supporting his conclusion.

Think of it this way: If the sales training system is working, what else should be true? Example empirical indicators that could corroborate Tom's claim might be the following: After the sales training program, (1) the percentage of initial prospecting calls that result in a sale increase; (2) reps follow up customers' inquiries quicker; (3) there are fewer customer complaints; and, (4) customers express a higher level of satisfaction with the sales force's performance. The more relevant evidence Tom can produce to support his claim, the stronger his argument will be that the training program actually affected sales positively.

Dealing with Affirming the Consequent

When a colleague confronts you with an argument that affirms the consequent, employ the following two strategies. First, simply point out that there are potentially multiple causes of "B"–the consequent of whatever "A" is. Second, help your logically challenged friend think through the following question: If A is true, what else should be true in addition to B? If you can't think of anything, then maybe A is false.

Remember, antecedents don't necessarily guarantee consequents. Correlation is not causation.

Bad Reasons

Location: McDonald's headquarters.

Issue: How should the corporation reinvigorate coffee sales in Australia? (Note to any McDonald's employees: this is an apocryphal interpretation of a case study found in Byron Sharp's textbook, *Marketing: Theory, Evidence, Practice*.)[1]

Ethan (vice president, marketing for McDonald's Australia): *"So, Emma, your team was charged with coming up with a strategy to revive our coffee sales. What is your team's recommendation?"*

Emma (product marketing manager): *"We concept tested a new idea, Ethan, based on an image study we did on our brand last year. Our team does not feel that we can ever be a serious competitor to Starbuck's if we try to continue to sell premium and sophisticated coffees in our current channel of McDonald's restaurants. Our restaurants just don't have a premium or sophisticated image—face it, we're a fast-food restaurant. Consumers just don't link premium coffees with our restaurant brand. We believe that we need to break out with a totally new channel—a new retail outlet, with a new name, and image."*

Ethan: *"No way that's going to work, Emma. Other retailers have sold premium brands without creating a new channel and store brand—heck, you can buy a high end model of a Maytag washer and dryer at Sears; and even Kohl's department store sells the Ralph Lauren brand. No way. We just have to figure out how to sell a premium coffee in our existing restaurants."*

Emma: *"I see your point."*

Clearly, Emma did not make the best argument for her recommendation. For example, she might have conducted a research study on the proposed McCafé concept—and had it received a positive reaction from target consumers, she could have used those results to support her team's recommendation. Ethan is using her poor argument to conclude that Emma's team's recommendation is no good.

Definition: *Bad Reasons* is a formal logical fallacy in which "a conclusion is false because an argument given for it is bad."[2] Its logical form is as follows:

- Premise: Argument P for conclusion Q is bad.
- Conclusion: Therefore, Q is false.

Discussion

This fallacy most likely manifests itself in a group setting when several people are debating the goodness of one or more arguments. The motivation behind using the Bad Reasons fallacy is simply this: If a person can show that another's argument is poor or weak, that fact can be used to bolster one's own argument. As Gary Curtis says on his website, Logical Fallacies:[3]

It is always tempting, in the heat of debate, to think that one has established one's own case when all that one has succeeded in doing is undermining the opposition's case. To commit the Bad Reasons Fallacy is to act as though argumentation is a zero-sum game in which, if the other side loses, then you win.

Dealing with Bad Reasons

Don't put yourself, or your team, in a position in where a colleague can leverage your poor argument to his or her advantage. One way to accomplish this is not to present your recommendation as an argument—that is, as a well-thought-out set of statements comprised of premises and a conclusion designed to persuade others to accept it. Rather, offer your idea as a suggestion that will take some time and research to investigate. Only when you are ready to defend your argument should you present it to others for critique.

If you read Sharp's case study, you'll discover that "Emma's recommendation" turned out to be a grand success. Now, take a break from reading our book and go to your local McCafé and have a good cup of coffee.

Illicit Major

Location: Office of the VP of HR in a large vehicle parts manufacturer.

Issue: The VPs of HR and sales are discussing the criteria for hiring new salespeople.

Jacqueline (VP HR): *"I understand that you've been doing some research on your sales force and you'd like the HR department to screen applicants differently than we have in the past. What's your recommendation?"*

John (VP sales): *"This is what we discovered. Nearly all MBAs with bachelor's degrees in business have performed well as sales people. Also, in reviewing past applications, few undergraduate humanities majors have MBAs. So in the future don't pass on to us any humanities majors. They likely will not make good salespeople, and interviewing them is mostly a waste of our time."*

Jacqueline: *"That makes sense to me. Plus, it saves both your department and mine valuable time we can invest elsewhere."*

On the surface, John's argument seems to make sense, but it is not deductively valid. The truth of his premises—(1) that nearly all MBA's with bachelor's degrees in business are good salespeople and (2) that few undergraduate humanities majors have MBAs—*do not guarantee his conclusion*—that humanities majors lacking an MBA are not good salespeople—is true. This is an example of a fallacy known as "Illicit Major."

Definition: *Illicit Major* takes the following form:

- All A's are B's.
- No C's are A's.
- Therefore, no C's are B's.

You can see that the truth of the premises does not guarantee the truth of the conclusion in the following popular example of this fallacy:

- All cats (A) are mammals (B).
- No dogs (C) are cats (A).
- Therefore, no dogs (C) are mammals (B).

Discussion

Attributed to Aristotle, deductive arguments containing two premises and a conclusion are called *categorical syllogisms*. The two premises are composed of a general statement (called the major premise) and a specific statement (called the minor premise), such that the truth of these premises guarantees the argument's conclusion. The most famous of these is: All men are mortal (the general statement); Socrates is a man (the specific statement); therefore, Socrates is mortal (the deduced conclusion).

In Illicit Major, no statement is made that relates B to C or to not-C. Consequently, some not-C's could be B's. In our example, some undergraduate humanities majors without MBAs might just be good salespeople!

In reality, John may realize this, but he simply wants to "play the probabilities"—undergraduate humanities majors without MBAs just don't seem the type to be good salespeople. But accepting conventional wisdom disguised in an Illicit Major may blind you to valuable opportunities. Consider:

- All tech company employees (A) are tech-savvy (B).
- No high school-only graduates (C) are tech company employees.
- Therefore, no high school-only graduates are tech-savvy.

Dealing with Illicit Major

Google wants to hire tech-savvy employees; however, after extensive data analysis, Google's senior vice president for People Operations, Laszlo Bock, says that relying on college transcripts and standardized testing is not predictive of Google employee success. He says:

> One of the things we've seen from all our data crunching is that G.P.A.'s are worthless as a criteria for hiring, and test scores are worthless—no correlation at all except for brand-new college grads, where there's a slight correlation. Google famously used to ask everyone for a transcript and G.P.A.'s and test scores, but we don't anymore, unless you're just a few years out of school. We found that they don't predict anything.

> What's interesting is the proportion of people without any college education at Google has increased over time as well. So we have teams where you have 14 percent of the team made up of people who've never gone to college.[4]

Google understood the error of the Illicit Major, and it has changed the way it hires employees as a result. So, in dealing with this fallacy, remember Google!

Illicit Minor

Location: Conference room at Advanced Technologies' advertising agency.

Issue: How to best target web advertisements for the company's products.

George (Advanced Technologies' advertising department director): *"Jill, your agency has been tasked to research the best ways to target prospects with web ads for the new product. What have you come up with?"*

Jill (the agency's research director): *"We discovered several factors that may play a role in targeting the best prospects. As you'd expect, all consumers in the Progressive Segment are prospects for the new product.*

George: *"That's what we were hoping for. With our web analytics tools, we can identify the people who visit certain web sites and whether they fit our Progressive Segment profile or not. What else did you learn?"*

Kelly (the agency's research manager): *"We discovered that all prospects are families with at least two children in the household. So, based on what Jill said, we can safely assume that all two-plus kid households are in the Progressive Segment, and our web analytics can easily ID these particular households as well.*

Kelly may be correct, but her conclusion that all prospects are families with at least two children in the household is not a deductively valid statement. Let's explore why.

Definition: *Illicit Minor* is a formal logical fallacy that takes the following form:

- All A's are B's.
- All B's are C's.
- Therefore, all C's are A's.

However, some C's may not be A's.

Discussion

Let's examine Jill and Kelly's argument more formally:

- All consumers in the Progressive Segment (A) are prospects (B).
- All prospects (B) are households with at least two kids (C).
- Therefore, all households with at least two kids (C) are in the Progressive Segment (A).

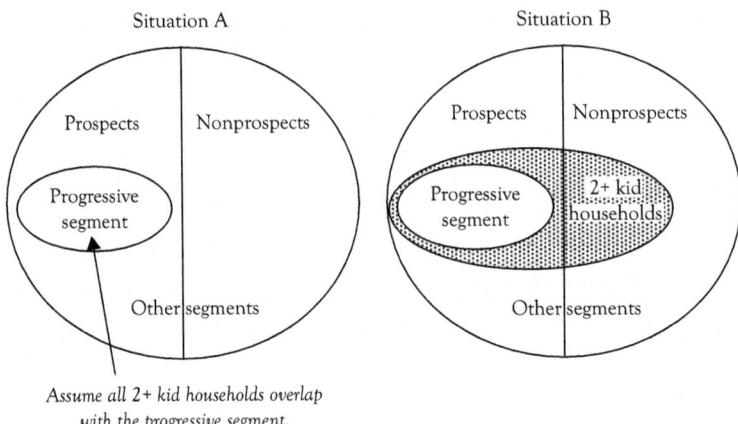

Assume all 2+ kid households overlap
with the progressive segment.

Figure 4.1 Two situations that are consistent with Jill's argument

What Kelly said certainly seems reasonable, but Jill's statement that
"All consumers in the Progressive Segment (A) are prospects," does not mean
that all prospects are exclusively in the Progressive Segment, which, if they
were, would make Kelly's statement correct.

At least two vastly different situations are consistent with Jill's argument, as shown in Figure 4.1. In both Situation A and B, all Progressive
Segment members are two-plus kid households; however, in Situation B,
most two-plus kid households *are not* prospects!

Dealing with Illicit Minor

We believe that the best way to deal with this fallacy is simply to restate
the chain of logic back to the person who made the argument. Another
useful tool can be to draw a Venn diagram giving a counter example to
the argument, and asking (using our previous example): *"What evidence
do we have that supports Situation A versus Situation B? Which is more plausible? Is there another interpretation to the relationships among the Progressive
Segment, prospects, and households with two-plus kids that is a more accurate
description of this market?"*

Sometimes the best way to understand a logic problem is to draw a
picture of it.

Negating Antecedent and Consequent

Location: In the kitchenette next to the coffee machine. You know, the one near the large conference room on the third floor.

Issue: How should we be looking to execute a new e-commerce channel partnership with our dealers?

> Don (sales leader): *"Most of our competitors let their dealers maintain a web site where they can conduct both product and service transactions with their customer base. Clearly it has proven to be a good way to compete since it has become such a standard practice in our industry."*
>
> Julio (marketing leader): *"I want to propose we put in place some different mechanisms to control this channel. I think we should front-end the transaction with our own site and then either pass the sale on to the dealer if they have stock or drop ship it and give the dealer a commission on the sale."*
>
> Don: *"Our competition is not doing it that way, so I have to assume it is not a good way for us to compete."*
>
> Julio: *"Wait, I think you have your logic mixed up."*

Julio is pointing out a logical fallacy known as "negating antecedent and consequent."

Definition: In *Negating Antecedent and Consequent*, say that someone proposes: *"If X is true, then Y is true."* If this is, indeed, a valid statement, then the following proposition is false: *"If X is not true, then Y is not true."* Y may be true for other reasons, even if X is not true.

For example, assume the following statement is valid: *"If it rains (X), then the sidewalk is wet (Y)."* Then the next statement is not valid: *"If it does not rain (not-X), then the sidewalk is not wet (not-Y)."* It may not be raining, but I could be watering my lawn, which makes the sidewalk wet.

Assume that *If X, then Y*, is a valid statement.	
Then, this transpositional form **(a)** is also valid: (a) *If not-Y, then not-X.*	But, this transpositional form **(b)** is not valid: (b) *If not-X, then not-Y.*

Let's see how this logical fallacy tripped up Don.

Discussion

Don's underlying logic is as follows: *"If X (competitors are doing what he describes above), then Y (it's a good way to compete)."* Julio offers an alternative strategy—"not-X"—and states that it, too, is a good way to compete.

However, Don then makes the illogical leap in critiquing Julio: *"If Julio's strategy is not-X"* [that is, it is not the same as mine], *then it is not a good way to compete."* Don unconsciously used the transpositional form **(b)**, which is not valid. Again, it is not valid because there may be other "good ways to compete" that differ from Don's "X."

Dealing with Negating Antecedent and Consequent

Julio has started off right by saying, *"Wait, I think you have your logic mixed up."*

However, Julio needs to further explain that, while Don's statement may be correct—and Julio does not dispute Don's statement—what it does not do is prove that something *untried* (e.g., Julio's idea) is not a good way to compete as well.

In short, *"If X, then Y"* is true, does not mean that *"If not-X, then not-Y"* is true as well. If the dog had not stopped to sniff the tree, he would have caught the rabbit, does not mean that if he had ignored the tree, he would have caught the rabbit.

CHAPTER 5

Informal Logical Fallacies in Marketing: Introduction

Unlike formal logical fallacies, you won't need a pencil and paper to draw Venn diagrams to identify these torturers of logic. Nonetheless, it's easy for them to fool us because, literally, there are hundreds (if not thousands) of them to be found on the Internet. With too many to memorize, our task to be good critical thinkers may seem insurmountable.

Not to worry.

All informal logical fallacies share one common property—they do not give you a good reason to accept someone's argument. This is because informal logical fallacies either don't give good evidence to accept an argument's conclusion, or the evidence they do give is poor, misleading, or irrelevant. In place of good evidence, informal logical fallacies often play on emotions—such as fear, hope, anger, belongingness, trusting, confidence, intimidation—as well as prejudice and conventional wisdom.

Additionally, one often includes an informal logical fallacy in an argument out of simple laziness. It's easier to make an appeal to emotion, for example, than to spend time trying to find good evidence for inclusion in a well-constructed argument.

We don't mean to imply by separating formal from informal logical fallacies that you might not be confronted with a situation in which both are used in the same argument. Often unintentionally, someone may make an argument using poor logic and then throw in an informal logical fallacy in the vain hope of strengthening one's case. Here's an example:

Formal logical fallacy: *Affirming the Consequent*	Argument content	Addition of the *Appeal to Popularity* fallacy to support the argument
If (P), then (Q).	If attending all industry trade shows is a good idea (P), then sales will increase (Q).	
(Q) is true.	Sales increased (Q is true).	
		Successful companies in our industry attend all industry trade shows.
Therefore, (P) is true.	Therefore, attending all industry trade shows is a good idea (P is true).	

This argument may be true, but it is not logically valid because the truth of the premises does not guarantee the conclusion to be true. Furthermore, the addition of the Appeal to Popularity informal fallacy may make the argument more appealing to one's audience, *but the fact remains that these are not good reasons to accept the argument's conclusion!* Just ponder the following for the moment: What *good evidence* does the person making this argument provide us to accept the claim that "attending all industry trade shows is a good idea"? Answer: None!

Among the literally hundreds of informal logical fallacies we researched for this book, the 54 that follow are the ones that most resonated with our marketing experiences.

Special Note

Our book's discussion of formal and informal logical fallacies just scratches the surface of this topic. Although the last chapter in this book provides a list of suggested readings, we also suggest you visit Gary N. Curtis' website www.fallacyfiles.org/.Gary holds a PhD, in philosophy from the University of Indiana and is a professional logician, philosopher, and writer.

Ad Hoc Rescue

Location: An advertising agency conference room in 2001.

Issue: Agency representatives are discussing with their client the need to move some portion of the company's media expenditures from television to the new "social media."

> Mary (client): *"We need to continue to invest 70% of our media dollars in television. Our sales have increased every year since we've advertised on TV, and we don't want to risk reversing this trend."*

> Jennifer (agency executive): *"But that rate of increase in sales has been dropping yearly, as you know, Mary. And research we have shows that consumers in your target market are spending more time on the Internet. We really need to address that in your media buy."*

> Mary: *"But, Jen, nobody really sees those Internet ads—they are tiny and don't have the same impact as seeing a television commercial on your TV screen."*

> Jennifer: *"But Mary, a significant portion of your target market—our research estimates 80%—records their favorite shows anyway, and they skip over the TV ads."*

> Mary: *"Then Jennifer we need to put more action in our ads to grab our audience's attention."*

Mary is clearly grasping at straws to justify her long-held belief that television advertising should continue to garner the vast majority of the firm's advertising budget. As the agency bases its evidence on hard statistical research, the client becomes more desperate to defend her original argument.

Definition: *Ad Hoc Rescue* is committed when a person tries to support his or her argument with weak or simply bad reasons and then responds to other arguments with explanations that have no evidentiary or logical support.

Discussion

Ad Hoc Rescue typically occurs when a person holds a belief that is shown to be false, to be logically inconsistent with other beliefs, or simply to rest on weak grounds. Think of this as "doubling down" with bad information. But all of us are human, and we know based on our experiences that many marketing and advertising executives were highly suspicious of Internet advertising in the early 2000s.

Imagine how often Ad Hoc Rescue must have echoed through the halls and conference rooms of GM during its transition out of bankruptcy. The board appointed two outsiders with no auto-industry experience as CEOs—AT&T's Ed Whitcare (2009–2010) followed by the Carlyle Group's Dan Ackerson (2010–2014). The board directed Whitcare and Ackerson to challenge the very assumptions and beliefs that eventually drove GM into bankruptcy.

In our vignette, when faced with evidence that her argument is weak, the client first responds by saying, *"But those Internet ads are tiny and don't have the same impact as seeing a television commercial on your TV screen."* This is a vacuous explanation primarily because the word "impact" is not defined and supported by evidence. When confronted with the fact that 80 percent of the target audience records TV programing and skips the ads, Mary feels that simply making better attention-grabbing ads is the solution. These ad hoc explanations are nothing more than rationalizations vacant of supporting facts or logic.

Dealing with Ad Hoc Rescue

Ad Hoc Rescue often reflects an emotionally charged reaction to having one's strongly held, even "cherished," beliefs contested. For this reason, you want to avoid not only using this fallacy yourself, but also putting someone else in a position of publicly defending a core belief.

Sometimes we simply don't think through our own rationale for accepting a strongly held belief because it's one that, over time, we've simply come to accept. To us, these are not "beliefs"—they are "facts." When we find ourselves in an uncomfortable situation in which our belief is challenged, we naturally react by thinking of explanations "off-the-cuff" to justify our position. This is why Ad Hoc Rescue is sometimes called Making Stuff Up, or the "MSU" fallacy. The best course of action in such cases is to mentally note the counter arguments made to your belief and, in some cases, defer the discussion by saying something like, *"You make good points. I need to re-think my rationale for the argument I just made and see if I can explain myself better when we revisit this topic at our next meeting."*

When colleagues (and especially superiors) engage in an Ad Hoc Rescue, do not embarrass them! Be conciliatory. Say something like, *"I believe I see what you're trying to say. Let's do this: Here are my primary questions about the statements you've made.* [Briefly summarize your objections, evidence, and logic in a follow-up e-mail]. *Next time, let's review all the evidence and reasoning on both sides of the issue and see if we can resolve our different points of view."*

Ad Hoc Rescue is often motivated by preserving one's dignity. Avoid it at all costs.

Ad Hominem: Personal Attack

Location: Engineering conference room in a small agriculture equipment products company.

Issue: Attendees are debating the product development cycle.

> Janet (marketing director): *"We have seen a negative trend in our new product sales ratio. This is the ratio of product sales released in the trailing 12 months to overall sales. Except in mature or secular declining markets, this is typically a sign of new products missing the mark. I think we need to stop working on what tickles our engineering funny bones and get better linkage of the product development pipeline to customer needs."*

> David (engineering director): *"What do you know about our product development cycles? You can't even make your Lotus Notes work."*

Janet has made a bit of a personal slight against engineers—probably a slight based on the stereotyped motives of engineers, and David has responded with a full-on personal attack against the marketing director in response to what might be a very lucid argument.

Definition: The *Personal Attack fallacy* (or ad hominem, Latin for "abusive") is one in which the antagonist makes an unrelated or irrelevant attack against the protagonist's person or character instead of attacking the argument.

Discussion

The salient feature of this ad hominem form is that it is a direct attack on the person's ability or character that is totally unrelated to the argument being made.

In the previous situation, Janet's slight of engineers is based on the stereotype that engineers often work on what they like to work on, rather than being guided by customer needs. This attack is not a direct personal attack on their character as much as it is a matter of guilt by association.

On the other hand, the "you can't even make your Lotus Notes work" attack by David is equivalent to saying, "You are stupid." This is a clear personal attack unrelated to the argument that the "new product sales ratio" is evidence that the product development pipeline has become disconnected from the customer needs.

Of course if the context is different from what we assume, and Janet really is a moron—for example, if David had recently e-mailed a study showing good linkage between his product development pipeline and customer needs—then this attack is not irrelevant or as personal as presented.

Dealing with Personal Attack Arguments

Not letting a personal attack stir up emotions is difficult. But for all the parties involved, it's best to move the line of discussion back to constructive logic. In the case outlined earlier, someone needs to say something like, "OK, let's be hard on problems and not on people." Or perhaps, with the right personalities around the table, deflect the attack with humor: "You think she has problems with Lotus Notes, you ought to see her hit her driver on the golf course." Another option might be to say, "It's clear that our new products are not selling as well as we would like. Let's direct our energy to defining and solving that problem."

There are many ways to get across the message that a personal attack is an unacceptable argument.

Against Self-Confidence

Location: A national grocery store's retail outlet in a major city. The senior vice president (SVP) of perishables marketing is meeting with the regional managers (RM) who oversee the meat department.

Issue: The managers are discussing the pros and cons of periodically offering shoppers cooked samples of meat products as a promotional effort to increase sales.

> Elizabeth (SVP): *"What I like about this idea is that it's a great way to introduce new meat-based menu items to our customers. After eating a free sample, the customer will be stimulated to try it at home."*

> John (Midwest RM): *"I know a lot of our competitors do this, but I'm not sure it really works. Most people come into the store with a shopping list. They know pretty much what they want to buy. If what we're sampling is not on their list, they likely won't buy it. And even if they like the sample, most will forget about it the next time they're putting together their shopping list or are in the store. All we're doing, Elizabeth, is giving away free product."*

> Elizabeth: *"How confident are you, John, that you're right … are you really sure?"*

> John: *"Well, I guess I can't really prove it."*

> Elizabeth: *"Then let's try it! This will be a great promotional program that we can push at different seasonal and holiday times of the year."*

Definition: *Against Self-Confidence*—sometimes called *ad fidentia* (literal translation, "to confidence")—is when one uses an admission of uncertainty about an argument to discredit it.

Discussion

Clearly, the SVP and the RM do not give any facts or data to support their views, although the few reasons they do give seem plausible on the surface. For example, Elizabeth claims that the sampling experience will "stimulate" shoppers to purchase more meat items. If shoppers like the sample, which is a presupposition in the SVP's argument, this claim seems reasonable. But John's claim seems reasonable too—shoppers typically purchase what's on their shopping list.

Elizabeth then employs the Against Self-Confidence fallacy, using John's lack of self-assurance to bolster her own argument. What makes a claim credible and worthy of use in an argument is not the confidence we have in the claim's truth—rarely is anyone 100 percent certain of anything in life, let alone marketing—it's the confidence in the evidence and logic we have to support our claim.

Dealing with Against Self-Confidence

This fallacy can arise in the following three situations:

- When defending your own argument, by getting colleagues to confess their lack of confidence in their arguments.
- When defending against this attack, by having to admit that you are not completely confident in your own assertions.
- When viewing this fallacy in a meeting among group members.

As a reader of this book, you can summarily deal with the first issue by simply not doing it! If you are on the receiving end of such an attack, be prepared to discuss some evidence that supports your claim. If you don't have those resources at your fingertips, acknowledge that your enthusiasm is insufficient justification for your claims and ask for some time to locate data that will address the issue at hand. You do not necessarily have to conduct a marketing research study to defend all your claims. You might find secondary research sources (e.g., on the Internet) that provide at least some justification for your propositions.

Finally, when you observe this fallacy being used by others in a group, consider taking the following actions: First, politely point out the fallacy that's being used and why someone's lack of confidence in a claim is not a good reason to discount that claim.

"I appreciate the enthusiasm you have for your position. But as we know, enthusiasm is not enough to turn a profit. Is there anything we can do to help

us justify your argument when we present it to others" (name other people in the organization, such as senior executives, that might question the proposition being made).

Second, offer ways to strengthen the claim in question, perhaps by seeking advice from acknowledged industry experts or conducting some kind of secondary or primary research.

The confidence one has or does not have in a claim is irrelevant to how good the claim actually is. "… [C]hallenge facts and logic, and not people."[1]

Alleged Certainty

Location: Product development meeting in a Fortune 500 company.

Issue: Marketing is making a final recommendation to Research and Development (R&D) to proceed with developing a new product.

> Harry (marketing executive): *"… and, in summary, our marketing research indicates this new product will fit our customers' needs and displace our lead competition—it's a slam dunk."*

> Jean (R&D executive): *"Looks compelling, Harry. What did your research say about customers in the EU—this study was just done in the U.S., correct? We have to make a global recommendation, not just U.S."*

> Harry: *"Well, Jean, we didn't have enough budget to do the same study outside the U.S. but, as everyone knows, customers for this product category in the EU behave exactly the way those in the U.S. do."*

How often have you heard a similar conversation in meetings you've attended? They often include phrases such as, "I think we can all agree …" or "We all know …". When you hear these words, your logic antenna should shoot up because you have just witnessed (but hopefully not propagated) a common logical fallacy known as "Alleged Certainty."

Definition: *Alleged Certainty* is a claim that presupposes its own truth, usually prefaced by statements such as "Everybody knows that …," "It is a universal given that …," or "We all know that."

Discussion

Often, the reality is that everyone does not know "that," and to assume that they do is putting forth a bad reason to support a proposition. Often managers use Alleged Certainty unconsciously because they really do assume that something is (or should be) obvious or common sense to all involved. For example:

"We can all agree that the Pacific Ocean contains salt water."
"Without a source of funding, the project cannot go forward."

Even when a statement is 100 percent correct, the speaker should be prepared to support her assumption, no matter how obvious it might appear to be.

Alleged Certainty is sometimes used intentionally. For example, a manager can use Alleged Certainty to sum up an argument and move the conversation forward; or he might use this type of logical fallacy to assert authority over a group and get his way.

Dealing with Alleged Certainty

Don't be guilty of using Alleged Certainty yourself. Don't frame a thought with words such as "Everyone knows ...," "It is certain that ...," or "We can all agree that ...." Leave some room for *uncertainty.* Try these alternatives: "I feel it is probable that ...," "It is likely that ...," or "I'd like you to consider that ...."

When you encounter Alleged Certainty in a business environment, try the following:

1. Although it is second nature to try to assess the speaker's intentions, don't. The logical "high ground" is to treat all Alleged Certainty as an honest attempt to state what the speaker feels should be obvious to all.
2. If the use is innocuous—has no bearing on the business—let it go.
3. If the use of Alleged Certainty has a potential for impacting the business, ask the speaker for supporting facts—in a way that does not appear to "grill" them. For example:

"That sounds logical to me; what's that based on?"
"That's a really interesting point—was anyone else aware of that?"
"That may well be the case, but do we have the data to support that?"

Alleged Certainty is a common logical fallacy that is relatively easy to identify and address—"everyone knows that."

Ambiguity

Location: Strategy meeting between the CMO and VP of sales of the Acme retail automotive service company.

Issue: The company executives are brainstorming a positioning strategy designed to motivate consumers to have their vehicle serviced at their retail service centers versus the vehicle manufacturers' service centers.

> Sylvia (CMO): *"We need to refresh our positioning strategy. Vehicle manufacturers are becoming more aggressive in getting their customers back to the dealer for service. I know that this behavior is hard to counter during the vehicle's warranty period, but there must be something Acme can do to attract consumers whose vehicle is out of warranty."*

> Jack (VP sales): *"If we can convince consumers that our service centers will exceed their expectations, that should motivate them at least to consider Acme, and some of them certainly will give us a shot. Therefore, I think we should consider a positioning strategy that incorporates this idea of exceeding customers' expectations."*

Definition: The *Ambiguity Fallacy* occurs when a claim is made that supports a conclusion, but the claim itself is ambiguous. Jack makes the claim that "exceeding customer expectations" will attract new customers to their service centers; however, the meaning of the term *expectations* is ambiguous.

Discussion

Expectations is one of the most ambiguous terms used in the field of marketing, which is ironic because it is also one of the most widely used. A Google search of "customer expectations" turned up nearly 18 million citations.

If Jack wants to exceed customers' expectations, what exactly does Jack want to exceed? Consider the following definitions of this term:

- *A forecast*: In this context, an expectation is a forecast of performance. For example, say a customer expects to wait 30 minutes to get his oil changed at Acme, and it only takes 20 minutes. In this case, the customer's expectations have been exceeded positively, which would relate positively to customer satisfaction and repeat purchase. If it had taken 40 minutes, her expectations would have not been met, which would relate negatively to customer satisfaction and repeat purchase.
- *A minimum performance level*: In this context, an expectation is based on the minimum acceptable level of performance before a customer starts looking for a different brand. In Acme's case, customers may begin getting irritated and start looking for another service operation if the wait time is much longer than 35 minutes.
- *Performance level that should be provided*: From this perspective, expected performance that *should* be provided is often based on what the product costs. For example, someone who purchased a Cadillac might expect to wait a shorter amount of time for an oil change than someone who purchased a Ford Focus.

If Acme wants to exceed customer "expectations," what definition do they use? The first definition, where "expectations" is construed as a forecast, is problematic to implement. For example, forecasts of performance are a function of past performance. If a customer always waits 30 minutes for an oil change, their forecast will be 30 minutes for their next oil change. If Acme exceeds that by, say, 5 minutes, and does this consistently, the new customer expectation will be 25 minutes. But to exceed that, Acme needs to reduce the wait time to less than 25 minutes. To exceed the customer's expectations consistently is impossible over time.

The second definition—minimum performance level—is problematic, too. Meeting a minimum performance level may put Acme at risk from competitors who offer faster service. Finally, imagine yourself to be a Ford Focus owner who consistently observes that, over time, Acme's customers who drive more expensive cars than you get faster service. Thus, defining expectations as the performance level that *should* be provided can produce unintended consequences.

Bottom line: Jack's recommendation incorporating the Ambiguity Fallacy is meaningless.

Dealing with Ambiguity

Challenging this fallacy is relatively easy because it does not involve questioning the person's knowledge or intelligence as overtly as with an Alleged Certainty fallacy, for example. Simply ask the person making the ambiguous statement, *"What do you mean when you say (insert ambiguous term or phrase)?"* When you come across the Ambiguity Fallacy, simply ask for clarification—no need to be ambiguous! Just be prepared to offer some alternative interpretations of the ambiguous term, if necessary.

Appeal to Accomplishment

Location: Board room of a national department store chain. The CEO, CMO, and various VPs are seated around the conference table.

Issue: Setting corporate strategy.

Ron (CEO): *"In summary, our strategy will be to have everyday low prices. We've got to wean the customer from all these sales and coupons and drop our 'high/low' pricing strategy. In order to differentiate our stores from the competition, we're going to have boutique stores-within-a-store—for instance, a location in the middle of the store where our female shoppers can get their nails done. And we're going to wrap up this new strategy with a new logo and just use our company's initials as our brand."*

Sandy (CMO): *"That's a major change from what we've done in the past. Why do you think it will work?"*

Mary (VP merchandising): *"Yes, none of our competitors are doing that? Although I see how it will make us different, I don't understand why it will work."*

Ron: *"Just look at my track record … I reinvented the retail store at Apple, and I was the VP of merchandising at Target when its clothing lines broke all previous sales records. Trust me, this will work."*

Sandy: *"How about conducting some marketing research and getting the customers' reactions to these ideas?"*

Ron: *"Sandy, we didn't do marketing research at Apple!"*

Although the previous conversation is apocryphal, the situation, proposed strategy, and name of the CEO are real. It's part of Ron Johnson's story during his 18-month reign as CEO of JC Penney, which he rebranded JCP. Ron appealed to his accomplishments at Target and Apple to justify his transformational, but failed, strategy at JC Penney.

Definition: *Appeal to Accomplishment* is a logical fallacy in which an argument is shielded from analysis based on the accomplishments of the person making the argument.

Discussion

The Appeal to Accomplishment has allure to the person making it. First, it's an ego trip to refer directly or indirectly to one's accomplishments. Second, it can be used to squash any recommendation for further analysis of the situation and options that might shine light on the issue at hand, including conducting marketing research. For example, think of engineering leaders saying, "This is how we engineered the wildly popular Ford Mustang so we don't need to research and test its applicability here." Finally, it shortens the discussion and moves to action. But it was the downfall of JC Penney.

We're confident that you've seen this logical fallacy play out in your organization. The authors of this book certainly have experienced it, either as consultants or as senior executives of Fortune 500 companies— but we're hesitant to give personal examples because we're not interested in burning any bridges!

C-suite executives are not the only ones guilty of appealing to this logical fallacy. Often the people reporting to them are hesitant to question their senior executive's arguments. This seems to happen for one of two reasons. First, it's prone to happen if the senior executive has a large ego and is not receptive to constructive criticism. Second, it can happen if the senior executive is extremely articulate, has a dynamic personality, and a positive, get-it-done attitude that inspires employees to the point of being led like sheep. *"It sure did work for him at Apple and Target; let's hope it works for us here." "Isn't his willingness to shake things up around here energizing?"*

Prior accomplishments per se do not support a new argument, especially regarding a new or different situation. Only when a person's accomplishments are *directly* related to the argument being made might they offer justification for a given point of view. So, although Ron Johnson had a successful career at Target and Apple, the case could be made that those experiences did not completely transfer to JC Penney's situation.

Dealing with Appeal to Accomplishment

Personal experience tells us that this fallacy can either be difficult or easy to deal with.

If it's brought about by a senior executive with a big ego whose motto is, "It's my way or the highway," then unfortunately there is not much you can do, other than try to protect yourself from the outcomes of the executive's bad decisions.

In contrast, if the perpetrator of the Appeal to Accomplishment simply enjoys being recognized for his past accomplishments and is open to constructive criticism, then you need to employ your best human relations skills in bringing the argument under closer scrutiny. Here are some suggestions:

- Recognize the person's accomplishments.
- Enlist the support from other affected parties so it is not just you against the boss.
- Ask something like, *"How can we build on your experience to increase the likelihood that your argument is correct?"* Or, *"How can I help you build a stronger case for your argument? There may be others involved in the decision who don't appreciate the experience you bring to the table."*

- If possible, point out past company experiences where Appeal to Accomplishment did not work. *"You might recall when Kyle, in engineering, had this great idea for a small boat engine based on his experience at the Honda Lawn Mower Engine Division. It sounded good at the time, but that small boat engine never met our sales targets. Post mortem we found that the neat features that benefitted lawn mower owners did not deliver the benefits that boat owners valued. We should have done some additional thinking before we made the assumption that, just because Kyle had made a killer engine in the mower business, his ideas would work the same in marine."*

As with all logical fallacies, the best advice is not to commit them. Perhaps Ron Johnson's tenure at JC Penney would have been longer if he had the humility of professional soccer player Mia Hamm, who said: "Many people say I'm the best women's soccer player in the world. I don't think so. And because of that, someday I just might be."[2]

Appeal to Authority

Situation: Communications planning meeting in a midsized company.

Issue: Attendees are discussing media mix for an upcoming product launch.

Cindy (marketing director): *"We need to decide just how much social media to use in the launch."*

Jack (ad agency account executive): *"Well, Cindy, we think you need to commit heavily to social media. Here's an article from* USA Today *showing that companies your size are spending more and more on social media and less on print."*

Lynn (sales manager): *"I talked to the sales manager at Allied, and he said they are going to use a lot more social media this year, too."*

Cindy: *"That's interesting, Lynn, but Allied isn't really in this market, is it?"*

Jack: *"Bottom line, Cindy, our media manager is really suggesting increasing the amount you spend on social media and cutting print."*

The preceding discussion has been common in meeting rooms across all types of companies over the past several years. Notice that the media mix decision is being fanned by the suggestion that not one, but *two* authorities are endorsing the claim that more social media is needed— *USA Today* and an agency media manager. This is a clear-cut case of the logical fallacy known as "Appeal to Authority."

Definition: An *Appeal to Authority* is being made when the veracity of a claim is made by appealing to an "authority" who says your claim is true. Such an appeal is fallacious if the source is not truly an expert.

Discussion

Appeals to authority are common in marketing because of all the outside advice companies receive from marketing and advertising consultants. In the case of social media, this seems to be even more the case because many middle-aged marketers are unfamiliar or uncomfortable with this new advertising medium. Reaching for or deferring to the support of an "expert" is common.

What's more, with the growth of the Internet, the ease with which people can position themselves on social media sites (e.g., LinkedIn, Facebook, Twitter) as authorities has resulted in an exponential growth in the number of "experts" in almost every field—marketing being no exception.

Recognizing an Appeal to Authority is generally easy, at least to the person on the receiving end. In a simplified sense, we are being asked to believe something, "because THEY said so."

This logical fallacy is often less obvious to the people making an Appeal to Authority, usually because they have accepted the authority of the person (or source). They have gone through an internal (and unconscious) validation process, which leads them to believe the authority in question and accept it as fact. However, you can probably also think of cases where an Appeal to Authority was made by someone trying to "sell" a position by supporting it with an "outside expert."

Since marketers cannot be whizzes in all the fields that inform marketing—marketing research, marketing communications, sales management, behavioral economics, psychology, and so on—we sometimes have to rely on authorities when making decisions. But what authorities should we believe?

Dealing with Appeal to Authority

What, then, differentiates a good versus a fallacious Appeal to Authority? Here are some imperfect but useful guidelines:

- Is the expert specifically named? The vague *USA Today* example does not give enough information to judge the veracity of the claim.
- Is the authority a recognized expert? Indicators of recognition can be graduation from a well-known university, conference presentations, and past successful (and citable) consulting engagements.
- Is the expert an outlier? Are his or her views generally accepted in the relevant field of study? This does not mean that someone with a novel view in a given subject area is not to be trusted. The less mainstream the expert's views, however, the more scrutiny we should exercise in evaluating his or her credentials.
- Is the expert unbiased? Experts who have a broad portfolio of services and methods can be more objective in making recommendations. Exercise caution in appealing to "one-tool" authorities.

The next time you are prepared to make or are witness to an Appeal to Authority, ask yourself the aforementioned questions. An Appeal to Authority can be highly appropriate *if* the expert used is truly an expert to more than just the person making the appeal. Clearly, the better able an expert or source can offer empirical evidence for a *particular* claim, the better.

The social media decision? We'll leave that to the experts.

Appeal to Common Belief

Location: Partners meeting in the offices of a small venture capital (VC) fund in mid-1997.

Issue: Partners are discussing potential investment in a fledgling dotcom company.

> Dianne (managing partner): *"I don't understand how Diapers.com is going to turn a profit. I just can't see investing in any company that can't show how it's going to make money for five years."*

> Keri (junior partner #1): *"I agree with you Dianne; however, all of the other VCs in the area are dropping big money in these dotcoms. They have the resources to do the analysis. They must know something we don't."*

> David (junior partner #2): *"There are tons of online companies popping up, and all of them are getting funding—from someone other than us. If we don't make this investment, Dianne, we run the risk of being considered too conservative to play in this market.*

> Dianne: *"Ok. If all of our competitors are making these types of investments, I guess, David, it makes sense that we do too. Let's get in on Diapers.com's Series-A round at $10 million?"*

Oh, to have been a fly on the wall in Silicon Valley VC firms during the run up to the dotcom bubble bursting. For every Amazon.com and Ebay there were multitudes of Diapers.coms that received millions of dollars in private equity funding, and most of them failed.

Although we cannot say for sure, it looks as if the VC firms during that period were falling prey to a common logical fallacy, "Appeal to Common Belief," otherwise known as the "bandwagon effect." The poster boy for these dot-com failures is Boo.com, an apparel firm launched in the fall of 1999 that burned through $135 million before going bankrupt in May 2000.[3]

Definition: An *Appeal to Common Belief* is being made when something is purported to be true because most or many people in a particular group believe it is true (or behave as if it were).

Discussion

In marketing, an Appeal to Common Belief usually occurs in situations where someone is advocating support for a "thing" or "idea." How often have you literally been told that "we need to get on the bandwagon" in support of this or that? Some cases similar to the example given earlier involve a relatively small, select group (Silicon Valley VCs). Others involve appeals based on what the "masses" appear to be doing or believe in. ("There is no future for small, locally owned retailers—everyone buys everything at Walmart.")

It is easy to see in retrospect that even if all Silicon Valley VC firms *were* investing in dotcoms in 1997, doing so was not unilaterally a good decision. In real time, it can be more difficult to identify these fallacies, especially if there is at least some angst that "maybe others know something you don't." However, the claims that large numbers of people, or a large percent of a relevant group "all believe something" or "act in a certain way," should make you flash back to your mother's response to your childhood claim that "all of your friends are doing it." And it should motivate you at least ask a few questions.

Dealing with Appeal to Common Belief

As Sargent Friday of the TV show and movie *Dragnet* said, "Just the facts ma'am."

As with many logical fallacies, finding facts to address the Appeal to Common Belief is the way to salvation. How do we get the facts? Ask a few questions.

- If the issue is important, it is imperative that the stated group belief or behavior be *confirmed as fact* or at minimum, highly justified. If, indeed, it is proven to be hearsay (or repackaged second- or third-hand accounts), this must be exposed and discussed, but do so gently.
- Do the individual or group members appealing to common belief have the necessary knowledge or skill to provide insight on this topic? Although there is Wisdom in Crowds (a nod to author James Surowiecki),[4] not all crowds have the requisite information needed to provide useful insight on a given topic.
- What is the motivation of the person making the Appeal to Common Belief? As with most fallacies, it could just be

an honest mistake. However, it is worth at least considering what the person stands to gain from getting you and others to support this belief.

- Simply ask "Why" five times. Why is everyone following? Why? And Why? And Why? Oh, and Why? This will get you to a root cause. And "just because" is not a valid answer. See the Think Better piece on The 5 Whys.

So your mom's response remains: "If all your friends jumped off a cliff, would you do it too?"

Appeal to Consequences

Location: Chief of staff's office.

Issue: Determining a variable compensation factor figure for the senior staff.

Chad (chief of staff): *"Two years ago we set a strategic goal of increasing market share in Latin America by three points. This makes up a quarter of our two-year strategic incentives plan calculation. I'm putting together the calculation Sean (the CEO) is going to submit to the chairman. We increased our share three points, didn't we?"*

Mike (strategy director): *"Well, it's hard to tell in that market. The best market data sources change just about every year. It is pretty hard to come by a calculation with great accuracy, timeliness, and repeatability, so it really depends on what assumptions you are willing to use. If I calculate it one way, market share is flat, but if I use another method, we have moved up over three points."*

Chad: *"Well, that's a tough market with a lot of competition, so holding our own by one measure and going up by another is the positive result of doing some good work down there. I'd like to conclude that we have gained those three points of share so we can say we accomplished that long-term strategic objective and reward people for the hard work."*

Chad has chosen to believe one of the market share calculations because he likes the consequences of the calculation.

Definition: *Appeal to Consequences* is the logical fallacy of selecting the conclusion of a line of reasoning based on the desirability or undesirability of the consequences.

Discussion

In the preceding example, Mike acknowledges that the data might be unclear or even contradictory. He states that an argument can be made for the conclusion that the market share had gone up by three points. Chad seizes the opportunity to believe the results of the analysis because he likes the consequences of the result—rewarding people for their hard work. If Chad gets to reward not only the Latin American management, but also himself and Mike, this illustration would also reflect a conflict of interest.

Appeal to Consequences and wishful thinking are similar. They could be intertwined and might be reinforcing. The defining point between the two is the human nature driver—people choosing to believe in a potentially false argument because of the perceived/believed output (Appeal to Consequences) versus people wishing the input were true (wishful thinking).

In the previous illustration, Chad does not particularly change his judgment or acceptance of the input market share calculations. He just chooses to believe (today) in one set of inputs because it gives him the desired output. The Latin American managers making the market share calculations (and possibly Mike) might be accused of wishful thinking because they want to believe in the inputs as a real and meaningful output of their work.

Dealing with Appeal to Consequences

Look for the weaker side of human nature in an argument's premises by asking these questions: Are we just making a conclusion and need the work to prove us right? Did we already decide what was going to happen and are now fishing for research that supports the decision? Do people like the decision and, therefore, choose to believe the research and analysis?

Scratch the surface. Discover if the inputs and the process used to arrive at a course of action is valid, confirmed, and believed in.

Beware of the consequences. You may get what you want today, but if an Appeal to Consequences torches your logic's argument today, using the same "rationale" in the future may come back to bite you. Maybe Chad should have said, *"Sure we can believe this market share today and get what we want, but what happens when the company invests another $10 million in this market and the share target goes up another three points, and we can't deliver?"*

Don't appeal to consequences. Appeal to good arguments.

Appeal to Desperation

Location: Teleconference on a strategic improvement initiative.

Issue: Determining what to submit for a quarterly report.

Shyham (strategic initiatives manager): *"Paulette (the president) selected these initiatives and asked for quarterly updates."*

Dwayne (customer service manager): *"Yes, but during the past quarter we have not worked on the first one and, from what we learned on initiative number two, the path forward is not really as clear as we thought it was, so we need more work on it."*

Shyham: *"Well, we have to submit a report, and you know how Paulette hates anything but greens on the stoplight chart. I think you really are not giving yourself enough credit. What we should do is code these green, outline the work as in-progress, and mark it subject to future updates."*

Dwayne: *"Well, OK, that sounds like the only option."*

By appealing to desperation, Shyham has goaded Wayne into submitting a sugar-coated quarterly report.

Definition: *Appeal to Desperation* is the logical fallacy of selecting a course of action purely because something needs to be done:

- "Something has to be done!"
- "X is something."
- "Therefore, X has to be done!"

Discussion

It is rare in business that we are truly desperate and without options. It is wrong to approach any situation as having only one option, even if doing nothing is often an option.

A business can be in a desperate position or a person can be in a desperate position. Knowing the difference is important. Don't let the latter become the former. The aforementioned illustration was either a lack of personal preparedness or the desire to avoid being the bearer of bad news that created the desperation.

But businesses do truly face desperate circumstances at times. A business that has only two weeks of cash left and may not be able to pay the next payroll is in a truly desperate situation—for the business and for its customers and employees. In these truly desperate cases making sure the right option is taken can have the highest stakes.

Dealing with Appeal to Desperation

If it is a personal desperation then the solution set is often easier but less consequential for the business. The truth is always best in this situation. Unprepared, mistaken, not sure what to do? Take the "own up to it" option and not the "cover it up" option, which those around you may present as the only option in cases of personal or group desperation.

If what you are dealing with is truly a desperate business decision and you are presented with only one option, the first step should be to ask if it is really the only option. Get everyone to step back, study the inputs, study the outputs, study the process, "ask five whys," (see Think Better: The 5 Whys) and get more opinions. Admittedly, this is easier said than done because desperation usually comes with a short fuse. Do the best you can.

Regardless of the situation, rather than panicking and "doing something" out of desperation, construct a set of alternatives. To create these alternatives, you need to fall back on your training—apply lean principles, divide and conquer, trust in the judgment of subject matter experts rather than time-intensive processes, and don't let perfection be the enemy of the good. In the end, your solution may not solve your problems, and your desperate situation may explode, but at least everyone will know that even the best solution did not work.

Desperate times sometimes need desperate measures. This may be true, but employ the desperate measures in ideation, vetting, and selection—not in desperately placing your faith in the first idea that comes along.

Appeal to Emotion

Location: HR conference room of ACME, a privately owned, regional plumbing supply wholesaler.

Issue: It is July 2008, and ACME is faced with steadily declining sales. The company's management team is considering reducing the company's work force to lower expenses.

> Alan (ACME president): *"… so that's it—sales and net profits are down 25% versus last year, and there appears to be no end in sight. Housing starts are at a halt, and there is very little remodeling. I just don't see how we can get by without reducing head count."*

> Norm (sales director and Alan's brother): *"Al, I understand we are in trouble, but ACME has never had a reduction in force or even temporary lay-offs in the entire 90 years we have been in operation. Grandpa Bob made it through the Great Depression without having to cut staff. How will it look to dad and the rest of our family if we cut and run now? To our employees? To the local business community?"*

Definition: An *Appeal to Emotion* is used instead of reason to manipulate an outcome, most often to win an argument or position. Appeals to emotion can involve *any* emotion—fear, envy, hatred, pity, pride, anger, anticipation, disgust, joy, sadness, surprise, and so on.

Discussion

Appeals to emotion are commonplace in life. Perhaps the first time you were exposed to one was when your parents first noted that starving children in Third World countries would be lucky to have the liver and onions you were just served and rejected for dinner. Emotion is a powerful motivating force in nearly everyone's personal and professional lives. It is the fundamental premise behind marketing communications. Positive emotions are uplifting; negative emotions can be devastating.

The previous vignette is a good example of an Appeal to Emotion (pride in this case) that is being offered up in place of reason. Norm obviously disagrees with the need to cut staff, or he may be unwilling to face the negative consequences that accompany this move. Either way, his argument is not fact-based, but an attempt to play on his brother Alan's pride in the business. If pride didn't work, it is likely that Norm may have tried another emotional appeal (sadness? fear?) to get his brother to accept his position.

Appeals to emotion in business are fairly easy to identify, as long as you are not the one making them. They are arguments without relevant supporting facts or reason. Replay the appeal, and you will find nothing that gives a good, concrete reason why or why not to accept the argument. Appeals to emotion are also usually populated with "sensory" words, for example:

"How will that look to _____?"
"How will make you feel?"
"That just sounds so sad!"

Appeals to emotion are delivered in an emotional manner—raised voices for anger or disgust; low voices and bowed, shaking heads for sadness or pity. Body language can help you read the emotion.

As with any appeal fallacy, the intent of the person making it may be sincere or nefarious. Sometimes this is fairly transparent, but not necessarily. In the aforementioned vignette, Norm more than likely viscerally hates the idea of firing or laying off employees who are like family, or he is unwilling to endure the shame of being seen as the one who let the family business fail. However, if there were an accompanying backstory in which Norm was trying to use the situation to take control of the family company, you may reach a different conclusion.

Dealing with Appeal to Emotion

After identifying an emotional appeal, your first inclination likely will be to assess the reason for the appeal. Is it sincere? Is it an attempt to negatively manipulate or gain something undeserved? This, as we said, can be difficult to ascertain and, ultimately, may lead you astray.

The best approach is to ask questions to engage the party making the appeal and direct the discussion back to facts. The key is asking questions in a level, emotionally uncharged manner. Use a level voice and tone. Use nonjudgmental, nonthreatening body language. Don't accuse. Be empathetic. The preceding conversation may have continued as follows:

Alan: *"Norm, I can understand how you feel that way. I have had some of the same thoughts. What do you see as some alternatives?"*

Norm: *"I don't know Al. It will kill me to let any of our people go. I guess that's it. I know that we are in trouble—if we don't cut expenses, we can't continue to make payroll."*

This vignette was likely played out in thousands of business during the last economic downturn and hits a little close to home. One of us was involved in a downsizing that happened as a result of the 2007–2008 "recession." It's hard to remain objective when the outcome affects you very personally. However, removing, or at least tempering emotion with fact and reason in business decision making will consistently lead to better decisions.

Appeal to Extremes

Location: Weekly management team meeting in a regional grocery chain store.

Issue: The team is reviewing sales by category, including a newly introduced line of premade vegetarian meals.

David (produce director): *"So, as of the first month, sales of our Home on the Range Vegetarian Meals are 300% over forecast. There must be five times the number of vegans living in our market area! I think we should double the size of our organic vegetable cooler."*

Bob (store manager): *"That's quite a leap David. I think we better see how the next month goes first."*

David: *"Well I think we should dump all our traditional foods and just become an organic and vegan store! This proves there is no future in traditional foods."*

Definition: *Appeal to Extremes* is an argument taken to an extreme, absurd conclusion. It is also a form of a "slippery slope" fallacy. In fact, the Latin name for this fallacy is *reductio ad absurdum*—reduction to absurdity!

Discussion

While we are sure you have witnessed Appeal to Extreme fallacies *outside* the business world—political advertising is rife with them—we also assume that, as a marketer, you rarely have experienced arguments that are totally absurd. In fact, this fallacy was one of the more difficult ones we had to write. However, if you "dial it back a bit," the previous example is probably not that uncommon.

One person's absurdity may be another's reality. David, in the aforementioned vignette is willing to project his limited data to what Bob believes is an extreme end point. You have likely experienced some version of this in your career—a subordinate, peer, or superior who reached what you felt was an absurd conclusion from information that you jointly reviewed.

Think of the most radical positions your coworkers have put forward based on their interpretation of information, for example:

- Support (or lack of) for new products in development.
- Support (or lack of) for achieving business outcomes.
- Support (or lack of) for hiring decisions.

How can two or more seemingly intelligent people arrive at such varied interpretations? Why is David reaching such an "absurd" conclusion?

Sometimes, the person proposing the "absurdity" is simply floating a trial balloon—putting a straw-man in play. Or he might be using the extreme appeal to influence an outcome or start an argument. It is also possible that the person presenting an extreme appeal is simply naïve or inexperienced with respect to the subject at hand. But, in the previous vignette, what if you also knew that David is himself a vegan and most recently worked at a local Whole Foods store. What is your opinion about what David is proposing now? Do you assume that he is trying to "push a personal agenda?"

But what if you also knew that:

- Sales of organic and natural foods in Bob's store have been increasing at twice the rate of other foods for the last year.

- David has just received other survey data profiling the population in the store's market area which supports his claim on the prevalence of vegans living in the area (think Berkley, California).

Does having the rest of that information cause you to arrive at a different conclusion?

Dealing with Appeal to Extremes

Dealing with extreme appeals in the business world requires you to get to the root of the issue—the reason the person is making the appeal. This requires some detective work on your part but, unfortunately, the cycle time available for this is very short. In a group setting, such an appeal will be made and either accepted or attacked within a few seconds.

As suggested earlier, context is important in assessing whether an extreme position is warranted or absurd. Without full context, it is possible to arrive at incorrect conclusions about the intentions of the person making the argument. To ensure that fuller context is understood, try asking nonthreatening, open-ended questions to clarify the logic leading to the appeal. For example, Bob could have followed up with, *"David, that's an interesting conclusion. Tell me more about how you arrived at it?"*

Then Bob could have probed David's responses several times to get to a fuller understanding of the how the extreme position was arrived at.

Asking probing questions that get at the supporting rationale is also a good approach if you feel that the extreme position is an attempt to manipulate or start an argument, and even if you believe the position is being taken out of naivety.

Another option for dealing with an extreme appeal is simply to let it play out. Don't engage, but rather, let nature take its course and assume that the issue will reach a rational outcome. This requires some patience, and only works when the issue is not being addressed directly to you. But sometimes, a little silence can keep things from escalating, especially if you believe that the perpetrator may be trying to start an argument or influence an outcome.

In the meantime, eat your vegetables.

Appeal to Faith

Situation: Two business units of the Acme Boat and Marine Manufacturing Company have agreed upon a cooperative growth initiative with each other. One business unit deals with distribution and the other with manufacturing.

Issue: Should the new marine product be distributed through the manufacturer's own distribution channel (i.e., their own boat dealer network), or should it go through an independent marine/boat retailer?

> Dave (product manager): *"This current market is actually much different than most of our marine channel partners are used to."*

> Kevin (business unit leader): *"When we entered this initiative, we assumed that our channel [the manufacturers' boat dealer network] would bring more value than theirs [an independent marine/boat retailer] because, after all, marine is in our name and not theirs."*

> Dave: *"It's true that, on the surface, their channel seems too generic. But our channel partners are actually so specialized that they are not a perfect fit either. I think the actual success factor will end up being which channel can bring the investment resources to the table to acquire the capability and capacity we need to serve the boat owning customer."*

> Kevin: *"I think you have gone native after all that time spent with their side working out this deal. Our channel is the marine channel and therefore the right one to use. Have you lost faith in our channel partners? We will propose using our channel."*

Definition: An *Appeal to Faith* occurs when the conclusion drawn is deemed to be a fact, but it is based purely on faith, rather than evidence, analysis, or logic. In some ways this is similar to the situation in classical geometry where a theorem can be based on an axiom where axioms are decidedly self-evident—like faith is to some people—and do not need proof.

The logical form of Appeal to Faith is:

- The assertion that X is true.
- If you have (the right) faith, then you will see that X is true.

Discussion

The Appeal to Faith fallacy has similarities to others in this book, such as Alleged Certainty, Appeal to Common Belief, and Appeal to Tradition. What sets it apart from the others is that its abandonment of reason is solely justified by a specific (usually named) "faith." If you have this faith, you will believe the assertions. In the other afore-cited examples, illogical conclusions are based on tradition (even though most faiths have tradition) or believing what others commonly believe (even though most faiths have common believers), and so on.

In the previous example, Kevin's argument is tied to his "marine faith." He believes that because his channel is a "marine channel" that it is the right channel for *any* marine product.

Dealing with Appeal to Faith

Don't mix business with religion or politics. Blind faith in a "brand" or a commitment to "our side" is just like bringing religion or politics into business. Unfortunately, it may not always be your choice.

When dealing with people who hold a deep, committed faith, winning an argument is nearly as impossible as trying to change someone's religion or politics. So what do you do when someone thinks something is self-evident and you don't? Just like breaking any other logical fallacy, your weapons are the Socratic method along with data, analysis, examining cause-and-effect relationships, and tact!

The only route to success lies in illustrating that what was thought to be self-evident may not be. If you are successful, this will shake their faith (which, for them, may be disorienting or depressing, so do so with care). Dave could have pointed out the particular customer needs that need to be addressed in the cooperative growth initiative, what resources need to be brought to bear to meet those needs, and why the partner is in a better position to produce and manage those resources than Dave's and Kevin's company.

You must also consider the consequences in critiquing a person's faith. Imagine a company that has a large employee population with blind faith in its brand. This can be helpful in many ways; however, be mindful that, when you start dismantling the blind faith for one practical purpose, you do not crumble the morale of the whole organization. For example, Dave might explain how using the partner's distribution channel plays to both company's strengths, thereby enhancing both companies' brand equity in the customer's mind.

Appeal to Fear

Situation: Leadership meeting in the commercial side of a sports all-terrain vehicle distribution business.

Issue: Are we spending our marketing dollars in the right places? How are we going to pay for our need to move into new media and the new economy?

> Mike (marketing leader): *"We need to re-evaluate how we are spending our promotional budgets. Our competition has a much better new media presence. They are making a much bigger investment in all aspects of their online presence than we are."*

> Bertrand (sales leader): *"But if we reduce our trade show presence and spending, both direct and co-op with our dealers in trade rags, everyone is going to think we are going out of business. That will make it doubly hard to sell anything to consumers, let alone keep the dealers on board. Then we really will be going out of business."*

> Patrick (president): *"Well, don't expect to spend incremental funds. We need to limit our cost-to-sell to 13.5% of revenue. In fact we should be reducing that."*

> Mike: *"But today we are bringing a knife to a gun fight. We need to beef up our online spending."*

To make his point, Bertrand is appealing to fear—ignore his recommendations, and customers will "think we are going out of business!"

Definition: An *Appeal to Fear* occurs when a protagonist attempts to gain agreement by instigating fear, not through any supporting evidence.

Discussion

A notable characteristic about an Appeal to Fear is that it is often a desperate attempt to justify a conclusion when the protagonist is short on evidence. It is often used in conjunction with a slippery slope argument in which a domino effect of bad outcomes from bad to worse ensues if you don't accept the argument's conclusion. For Bertrand, this domino effect starts with (1) *"everyone is going to think we are going out of business;"* which leads to (2) *"it will be doubly hard to sell anything;"* and, finally, ends with (3) *"then we will really be going out of business."*

Fear operates on some pretty basic dimensions of vulnerability and severity. Typically appeals to fear arguments tend to describe a specific weakness that is perceived to be correct or believable (even if no evidence exists or is presented) and a bad but believable outcome (even if no causal link is established). On the surface, if you accept Bertrand's first premise, getting to the third doesn't seem all that unreasonable—except that premise (1) is unsupported!

When someone is using the Appeal to Fear argument, they will present something that looks like logic to create the following chain in the listeners mind: "If X happens then Y will happen and we don't want Y to happen because we are vulnerable to Y and Y is really bad." The protagonist is concentrating the argument on listeners' fears so they become emotional enough to ignore the simple question, "Are we sure that Y will happen if X happens?"

The use of fear could also be used as an order—*"Accept my argument or your job is in jeopardy."* The fear factor is used to control adherence to an order, which is similar to getting people to adhere to a belief in an argument, even if no evidence or reasoning (other than fear) are used.

Dealing with Appeal to Fear

As with almost all emotional appeals, the best response is to say, unemotionally, *"Are we sure that if X happens, then Y happens?"*

Probably you will not be able to leave it there. You will have to follow up with suggestions such as, *"Are there other possible outcomes or is Y the only one?"* or *"That is a place where we are vulnerable and, if Y happened, that would be bad. Is there something we can do to break the link between X and Y or create a new Y, an optional Y, which is actually a really good thing for us?"* In this light, consider what Mike could have said to Bertrand:

> *"You are absolutely right. We can't let our reduction in trade show space from 40,000 square feet to 20,000 square feet look like a loss for us or like a cost-cutting maneuver. This would definitely put us on a bad footing with both our consumers and our dealers. What I think we need to do is actually flip the event around. Let's downsize from 40k to 20k but put the spotlight on the release our new app at the trade show. Put twice as many people in the booth with a tablet in their hand showing how consumers can discover everything they need through the full life cycle of their product—including how they can buy parts and service from their favorite local dealer with extreme ease. So even though we reduce the size of the booth, we enlarge the size of our service capabilities. Our resized booth may not even be noticed."*

Appeal to reason, not fear.

Appeal to Novelty

Location: Sales leadership team meeting in a global electrical engineering company.

Issue: The sales leadership team is discussing the possibility of upgrading or changing its sales force integration software.

> Steve (regional sales manager): *"We have been using Sales Org for 10 years now and it's served us well. I vote we just buy their upgrade—it will be the easiest transition for our sales force to make."*

> Ephraim (sales technology director): *"Sales Tech is the way to go—it's the newest thing. Sales Org is old news—been around too long. This is a technology decision and with technology, new is just better."*

Definition: *Appeal to Novelty* is a common fallacy where something new or more modern is represented as being either better or an improvement on the current "thing" solely because of its newness.

Discussion

Everyone has experienced this fallacy firsthand (quick—which fallacy did I just use to make this point?). Okay, it is *likely* that *many* of you *may* have experienced this fallacy firsthand. Look no further than decisions made when buying computer operating systems; for example, the argument to move an organization to Windows Vista from XP or from Windows 8 from Windows 7. In the discussions we were part of, an Appeal to Novelty was one of the core arguments made in favor of the move. Sometimes new *is* better. For example, many of our clients who have continued to use Lotus Notes versus changing to MS Outlook have regretted the decision.

Appeals to novelty are common in decisions made regarding technology, probably because technology is a relatively fast-moving, ever-changing field. But this fallacy is far from limited to technology. One of the best examples of this is the "New Coke" debacle in the mid-1980s. "Classic Coke" was kicked to the curb because more participants preferred the taste of New Coke in blind consumer taste tests. However, when New Coke replaced Classic Coke on store shelves, consumers revolted, and the results have become a Harvard Business School case study on how not to make marketing decisions. We have seen numerous situations in the companies we worked for or advised where an argument for change was supported entirely (or at least primarily) based on the newness and, thus, perceived superiority of something.

With an Appeal to Novelty, the implicit assumption is that new is *better* than old. There is rarely anything nefarious about these arguments. People using this fallacy truly believe in their position and that what they're advocating will indeed improve the current situation. This could be that past experiences have led them to this belief, or perhaps they tend to be Innovators or Early Adopters of innovations (a thank you here to Dr. Everett M. Rodgers, and his *Diffusions of Innovations*).[5] However, in some cases, the person using this fallacy might stand to gain from the change and is using "newness" to motivate others.

For an argument to be an Appeal to Novelty, it must be made solely based on newness. However, in our experience, it is often combined with another popular fallacy—Appeal to Popularity (aka *everyone else* is doing it or the *market leaders* are doing it). The implications of these paired fallacies are that:

- X is new, Y is old. Therefore X is better than Y.
- Everyone else is doing X, therefore X is the right decision.
- And, if we don't do X, we will be left behind.

Dealing with Appeal to Novelty

New is often sexy and cool. But new is rarely the only choice and may not be the best choice in a given situation or a given point in time. Advocates of new things or ideas need to provide some proof that they are indeed better for some reason other than their "newness." The person supporting the new thing should be required to provide this supporting evidence. If he cannot provide this support, the idea should be tabled. Don't succumb to the siren song of "new" without doing due diligence first.

If an Appeal to Popularity is made in support of an Appeal to Novelty, as we described earlier, the argument can be even more difficult to withstand. Being perceived as "old" and "falling behind" are positions that many people try to avoid at all costs, personally and professionally. But if there is money involved (and there always is, directly or indirectly) good marketers owe it to themselves and their organizations to stand tall and ask for proof that new is better *and* that failing to adopt the new thing will put the organization at a disadvantage.

However, for the same reasons that new things should not be accepted without scrutiny, they should not be rejected out of hand just because they are new. Don't over react and throw out the baby with the bathwater. Give new things a chance to earn the right to supplant the old.

Final disclosure: This chapter is being written on a PC running Windows 7. No Windows 10 for me—at least not yet.

Appeal to Popularity

Location: Product development team meeting in a consumer healthcare products company.

Issue: The team is discussing possible line extensions for its mouthwash product, CLEAN & BRIGHT.

> Gene (brand director): *"So, to summarize, we have confirmed that our top two competitors—the market leaders—have just launched organic mouthwash products. We must do the same to keep up."*

> Rob (consumer insights director): *"How about we track the success of their new products for a couple months first? Our own research indicates a very limited market for organic CLEAN & BRIGHT."*

> Gene: *"That's all well and good, but if the market leaders have decided to go there, they must have data that supports their move. I have to believe they know something we don't."*

Definition: *Appeal to Popularity* is a logical fallacy commonly referred to as the "bandwagon effect." You may also have heard it referred to as "groupthink" or "herd behavior." Appeal to Popularity fallacies occur when the popularity of an idea is misconstrued to provide a stamp of approval for that idea.

Discussion

Appeal to Popularity is one of several fallacies that all three of the authors have experienced firsthand, some of us many times. Our own experiences with this fallacy range from decisions made about pricing, advertising, intellectual property, sales territory design, and product development. Indeed, the earlier vignette is a nearly verbatim recall of an actual meeting for a different type of product.

Compared to many other fallacies, an Appeal to Popularity is relatively easy to spot. It follows the form of "everyone is doing X, therefore X must be true." There are no other facts cited to support X, other than that the implicit or explicit assumption that "everyone" is correct.

Appeals to popularity can be intoxicating. Everyone likes to be popular right? But just like high school, just because the "popular" kids were doing something, doesn't mean it was the right choice (per your mother's advice).

Mistaking "popular" for "right" can be dangerous, but is easily done. In the previous case, the actions of the market leaders (the popular kids) are assumed to indicate the right direction, which is entering the organic mouthwash market. The pull is strong enough that the brand director is willing to disregard insights that were likely gained as a result of his own request. Assuming that the company's own data are correct, developing and launching the organic mouthwash will utilize time and money that should be spent on other new developments.

But denying the popular is often difficult. Our own experiences support the belief that when we have been successful, we *are* doing things right. The market leaders in this vignette may be companies that have been viewed as "doing everything right" in the past. Lesser shareholders often look at their market leaders with some deference (maybe not openly, but tacitly). The actions of market leaders are carefully watched for signs of opportunity or (hopefully) weakness.

Dealing with Appeal to Popularity

Just because appeals to popularity are easy to spot, does not necessarily mean that they are easy to head off. But they must be addressed quickly, before the bandwagon gets rolling. Calling out an Appeal to Popularity rapidly is necessary. Silence grants tacit approval that is difficult to recant later. Unlike some fallacies, where time helps to heal, this fallacy is best dealt with head on by more than one person. A solo voice trying to address an Appeal to Popularity can come across as negative or a naysayer, and his or her opinion will likely be discounted out of hand.

Since no facts are being offered other than "everyone is doing it," there is little to debate, other than *why* everyone is doing it. Try to move the group to examine why everyone is behaving in the specified manner. In the aforementioned vignette, the discussion might have taken this form:

Rob: *"I agree. The market leaders may know something we don't. They have obviously arrived at a different conclusion. However, before we begin our own development program, why don't we take a bit more time to reexamine our own data. Then we can observe how the leaders' first month or two in the market goes. We can't resource a new project until next quarter anyway, so let's use the time to learn why they are moving in this direction and how, perhaps, we may be able to beat them in the market."*

Buying some time for a more thorough evaluation of *why* everyone is doing something can be a good use of time. Popular ideas are not necessarily wrong ideas, but unless you understand why they are popular, you only understand part of the story.

Appeal to Possibility

Location: "War room" of a national consumer products manufacturer and marketer.

Issue: Brand strategists are debating plans for increasing the market share of one of their shampoo brands. To increase share, should they focus on increasing purchase frequency or market penetration?

> Conner (brand manager): *"The market our shampoo brand competes in is ultra-competitive. So Jackie, I just think we'll be better off trying to increase our brand's market share by getting our customers to use our brand slightly more frequently rather than trying to steal brand share from our competitors."*

> Jackie (CMO): *"Either way, Conner, it's not going to be easy. Certainly, if we try to steal share, we're going to have to increase our ad budget."*

> Conner: *"Regardless of the strategy, we'll need to spend more on advertising. Right now I'm thinking about the strategy for the campaign. I think we need a campaign to drive frequency rather than win new customers. The Nielsen data show that the customers of the larger market share brands purchase their brands slightly more frequently than do our customers. So it is possible to drive frequency. And if it's possible, I'm sure we can pull it off."*

> Jackie: *"Well, I can't think of any reason why your suggestion won't work. OK, let's develop a campaign aimed at frequency."*

Just because something is possible doesn't mean that it will be true. Moreover, "possible" is a vague term and begs the question, "How possible?" Future events with probabilities of occurring 1 percent and

99 percent are both "possible," yet the former is not likely to happen, whereas the latter is more probable.

Definition: *Appeal to Possibility* occurs when someone asserts that if X is possible, then X is likely to be true. But an Appeal to Possibility often appeals to other logical fallacies, directly or implicitly, for its justification.

Discussion

In the preceding example, Conner links his Appeal to Possibility to Nielsen data showing that larger market share brands are associated with higher purchasing frequencies. His stated premise is that increasing purchase frequency is something that the larger brands do through advertising and concludes that it is something they can replicate purely because it is possible.

First, Connor is correct in claiming that higher market share products have somewhat higher purchase frequencies.[6] However, he's incorrect in his direction of causation (the large brands advertised their way to frequency of use) and, thus, has inadvertently used the "correlation is causation" argument as justification for his Appeal to Possibility.

The interesting facts that Conner does not know (and have nothing to do with this fallacy) are that, generally, as market share increases so does "mental and physical availability" of the product. Compared to small-share brands, larger-share brands have higher consumer awareness and physical distribution causing a kind of "selection effect" in which larger-market share brands simply capture relatively more heavy users than smaller-share brands do.[7] So causality goes the other way—increasing frequency of product usage does not cause market share growth, but market share growth attracts heavier brand users. For more on this topic, see the Think Better section, "The Double-Jeopardy Law."

In addition to often invoking a false correlation–causation relationship, Appeal to Possibility often joins ranks with Appeal to Ignorance for its justification—"Well, action X is possible, *and no evidence exists that refutes my claim!*" (See discussion of the Appeal to Ignorance in

Chapter 1.) But as we discuss earlier in this book, lack of evidence is not evidence supporting a proposition.

The same is true when combining an Appeal to Possibility with an Appeal to Novelty. You often hear Appeal to Novelty when you go to a marketing conference. Someone is giving a talk about the latest and greatest "bells and whistles." Companies latch onto them because of their "novelty" and "possibility." What consultant Annie Zelm calls the "Grapefruit Diet Strategy" is one of these fads, in which a firm focuses on a single strategy—say social media—versus integrating multiple strategies to ensure product success. In general, there is an attempt to simplify, and this is how appeals to possibility and novelty combine—it is simple (and romantic) to assume that the novel approach is working by itself, not that it is part of a more complex mix. Without disciplined diligence to find the root cause through causal analysis, marketers often link the desire to believe in the novel with the desire to believe in possibilities and come up with a fashionable me-too strategy that most likely will not work. As discussed by Zelm:

> The grapefruit diet has been around for decades, but it seems we still haven't learned we can't live on citrus fruit alone. Nor should marketers rely entirely on a single marketing strategy while neglecting others. Some businesses lean so heavily on social media that they've significantly reduced their efforts in inbound marketing, public relations, email marketing, direct marketing and traditional advertising.

> Social media offers the obvious advantages of instant communication and direct engagement, so it's hardly a passing fad. That said, it's a mistake to assume your 50,000 Facebook "likes" are 50,000 likely clients, or that your target audience will find you on Twitter without being prompted to look. Social media is important, but, like all other tactics, it's just one element of a balanced marketing strategy. To be successful, you need to engage your audience across multiple channels online, in person and on paper.[8]

Dealing with Appeal to Possibility

Here are two thoughts on how to deal with Appeal to Possibility:

- *Don't use the word possible.* Use the word *probable.* In most cases, this is the more correct term. Most things are possible, but not everything is probable.
- *Investigate tacit assumptions.* Does an Appeal to Possibility implicitly assume another logical fallacy for its justification (e.g., Appeal to Ignorance or Appeal to Novelty)? Perform some due diligence of the causal link.

In the movie, "Dumb and Dumber," the beautiful and beguiling Adele Pichlow (played by Lauren Holly) tells the not so handsome and very dumb Lloyd Christmas (played by Jim Carrey) that he has only one chance out of a million of ever ending up with her. Carrey's character responds, "You're telling me there's a chance!" Chance. Possibility. The best marketing arguments lie in the realm of the probable.

Appeal to Ridicule

Location: Product launch team meeting in a national beer company.

Issue: The launch team (a multidisciplined group consisting of advertising, public relations, brand management, consumer insights, and sales management) is reviewing first-pass creative concepts prepared by the communications agency selected to assist in the launch of a new microbrew named *Portland.*

> Sally (agency account director): *"So that is what we propose to use for the initial Portland TV spot. Our testing showed this spot really appeals to males ages 18–30—our target audience. The images of young people doing fun things like hang gliding and white-water rafting really resonated with them. And the skateboarding dogs at the beginning of the spot broke through the clutter and grabbed their attention in a fun way."*

> Anne (advertising & PR director): *"I sat in on all of the focus groups and I agree with Sally, with a few very minor tweaks this campaign will be a success."*

James (sales director): *"Skateboarding dogs—why stop there? How about we do a whole series of ads using animals doing crazy stuff. If they liked skateboarding dogs, they will really love surfing bears or hang-gliding cats. Heck, we could even get some ferrets to play baseball. The possibilities are endless."*

(A tortured silence descends on the room.)

Definition: In *Appeal to Ridicule*, an argument is made to appear ridiculous by misrepresenting or exaggerating it in some way.

Discussion

Appeals to ridicule are common in political advertising, where candidates' positions are often misrepresented. However, we believe that, in today's organizations, this fallacy is fairly rare. Marketers have received enough soft-skills training that this type of nearly personal attack (albeit on an idea versus a person) is uncommon. However, we have experienced it—especially in situations involving "outsiders" such as communications agencies or consulting firms, where the receiver of the ridicule has to play nice or lose the business.

Although there may be some justification to use ridicule when an argument or position is worthy of it, this is an entirely subjective call. Well-used ridicule can help to diffuse a situation with humor and possibly win the audience over. Misplaced ridicule can cast the ridiculer as mean spirited, judgmental, simple-minded, desperate, or just foolish.

In our experience, when this fallacy is committed there is usually a relevant back story. The Appeal to Ridicule is a *result* of prior actions, discussions, decisions, or arguments rather than the *beginning* of them. For example, it is possible that James was not in favor of the communications agency that was selected for the campaign, disliked the campaign itself, or even believed that launching *Portland* is a mistake that would negatively impact his department. Whatever the reason, his outburst may have been his final attempt to keep something that he does not agree with (but that the team as a whole has adopted) from happening.

Dealing with Appeal to Ridicule

Appeals to ridicule are almost as easy to spot as skateboarding dogs. They are usually delivered in a harsh, judgmental "with us" or "against us" tone.

And often your first reaction is, "Wait, did he just say …?" Your first reaction may be to laugh out loud, or at least wait a few seconds and joke back. But the person delivering the ridicule is often serious, and this type of response is likely to escalate the discussion rapidly, and not necessarily in a way that leads to resolution.

The best way to deal with the ridiculer is to keep your cool; remember, he was the one who has made an error in reason, and not every comment deserves a response. A little silence can be golden in situations like this. It is likely that the ridiculer will be the next to speak and either recant or clarify his position.

Do a quick mental check to determine why the person is acting in this manner. If you clearly feel this is, as we proposed earlier, another in a series of actions or positions he has taken, address the deeper issue rather than the argument on the table now. That's where the problem lies. If, however, you cannot assess the reason for the ridiculer's position, it's time to tactfully point out that perhaps he may be taking the discussion in a less productive direction and ask good "why" questions to ascertain the reason for his position.

Meanwhile, sit back, open a bottle of microbrew (or your favorite beverage) and contemplate why no one has yet used surfing bears or hang-gliding cats in commercials.

Appeal to the Moon

If you are one of the 22 million people in the United States[9] or the one in four people in the United Kingdom[10] who believes that the U.S. moon landing is a hoax perpetrated by the U.S. government, you probably will not appreciate this logical fallacy.

Location: Advertising and communications department meeting.

Issue: What is standing in the way of getting the website up and running and driving $1 million in transactions by the end of next week?

Tom (sales and marketing leader): *"It is taking us too long to deliver results. I am under a lot of pressure to deliver this one ASAP."*

Ginger (marketing analyst): *"Well, it is not really as simple as it seems. We have a lot of pages to code and data to write and then re-validate. Not to mention, we still need to get the SEO algorithms worked out before we can actually turn on some industrial strength traffic promotion tactics intended to bring in the retail buyers and transactions."*

Tom: *"I don't get it. If we could put a man on the moon in 1969, why can't we get a simple shopping site up and running 50 years later? I can't accept these excuses."*

Tom is using an Appeal to the Moon to justify his time schedule.

Definition: *Appeal to the Moon* is really a bad analogy. In this case, it compares everything to going to the moon, a pretty amazing and difficult feat—therefore, everything compared to it seems easy and completely doable.

Discussion

Perhaps almost everything is possible, but not always probable. Sending someone to the moon is possible, but would not be probable without a lot of investment and brilliance. Even then it was risky, and each trip was not a sure thing (1.0 on the probability scale).

Dealing with Appeal to the Moon

Bring the audience back to earth. Work into the conversation terms such as "possibility," "probability," and "plausibility." It is great to keep a positive outlook on a situation but just because something is possible does not mean it is probable.

Ginger to Tom: *"You are right. This website is a lot easier to accomplish than landing a man on the moon but, like the moon shot, this website needs time, planning, resources and certain things to be done in a certain order. I would say it is possible we can go live when you want, but the probability is about 1 in 10 billion. Now, [Ginger is smiling] give me 100 times as many resources and I could get the odds down to 3 in 5.*

I have to assume that I will not get that 100x bump in resources? So, given our current plan, which matches our current resources, we have a 95% probability of delivering on time in 45 days."

Appeal to Tradition

Situation: The product and marketing research managers of a hardware tool manufacturing company are discussing a marketing research project.

Issue: What kind of exploratory research should be conducted prior to launching a quantitative study designed to help the company better understand how consumers shop for circular saws.

> Raechel (product manager): *"I want to execute a qualitative study before we jump into a quantitative study to help us home in on the right issues. So, what do you suggest we do for the qualitative phase of the study to help us understand how consumers go about shopping for and selecting a circular saw?"*
>
> Terry (marketing research manager): *"Focus groups—that's what we do before quant studies."*
>
> Raechel: *"I've been reading that focus groups are overused and that there are other ways to do exploratory research, such as one-on-one interviews, interviewing consumers at the point of purchase, even going shopping with consumers who are ready to buy a new product."*
>
> Terry: *"We've always done focus groups and they've always led to successful quantitative studies. They have passed the test of time."*

Definition: An *Appeal to Tradition* states that, because something has been done for a long period of time—"it's a tradition"—that it is somehow better or correct and that one should continue to do it.

Discussion

Making an Appeal to Tradition is a tempting way to support an argument, for several reasons. First, it's easy. Do what you've done in the past if it seems to have worked. After all, it's passed the test of time, as Terry defensively says in the aforementioned vignette. Second, you'll save time by not having to investigate or test alternative ways of doing something—we all know that free time is a scarce resource for marketing managers. Finally, it's just psychologically more comfortable not to stray too far from your comfort zone. Why take on added risk to try something new or different? Managers have enough stress in their jobs already.

This does not mean that the old ways of doing something cannot be the basis of a good argument if those old ways have *been challenged and tested over time*. In some cases, for example when product managers want to brainstorm with consumers, focus groups can be an excellent venue for such an investigation. You can brainstorm better with a group of 9 to 10 consumers around a table than you can with a single individual in a one-on-one interview. On the other hand, if the purpose of the research is not to brainstorm with consumers, but rather to investigate how individual consumers make individual purchases, one-on-one interviews are generally preferred. In the preceding vignette, Raechel suspects that Terry is making an Appeal to Tradition.

Using prior experience to make a decision falls into two categories. (1) The old ways have been challenged and tested for their validity over time, or (2) they fit comfortably within our skill set and utilize people, processes, and tools we can easily command … they are traditional. If the case is (1), then this is not an Appeal to Tradition. If the case is (2), then such an Appeal to Tradition is a logical fallacy.

Dealing with Appeal to Tradition

When someone makes an Appeal to Tradition, perhaps the first way to challenge it is to do so indirectly. Without hurting egos, partially agree with the person or group that is making this appeal. For example, Raechel might have said, *"Yes, Terry, you're correct that focus groups have served us well in the past and, with our limited resources, we certainly can't be running around trying to test every new research method that pops up."*

Second, following our example, Raechel might have reminded Terry of the study's ultimate objective and that there likely are multiple ways to achieve it. *"Just reviewing for a minute, we want to understand how consumers shop for circular saws. And we all agree that we need to conduct some kind of exploratory research on this topic before we launch a quantitative study.*

In this regard, the question we need to answer is, 'What kind of exploratory research will best help us meet our objectives?'"

Finally, Raechel should brainstorm with Terry to develop a list of exploratory research design options, go over the pros and cons of each, and let the evidence lead to the best solution. In our example, the "evidence" could be articles from recognized experts on the pros and cons of focus groups versus alternative exploratory research interviewing techniques. Raechel can easily find such a discussion in a college-level marketing research textbook.

There likely are some things that will never change because they indeed have passed the test of time, such as duct tape, Frisbees, and drill bits (evidence, statistics, and causal links support the conclusion that duct tape is a universal solution to many of *man*kind's problems). But when constructing arguments to support marketing recommendations, making an appeal to *untested* tradition may blind you to better ways of doing things.

Argument by Gibberish

Location: Apollo Corporation's conference room.

Issue: The chief marketing officer (CMO) called a meeting of all strategic business units' marketing personnel, together with some industry consultants, to discuss the future of the boating market—and Apollo's future strategy in it. Apollo manufactures boats and marine engines.

Jerry (CMO): *"What can we do different at the boat shows to attract first-time buyers? If we don't expand the boating market, it's going to be very difficult to grow in the future."*

Abbud (marketing manager, Haven Boats): *"We need to take the blinders off and pursue a holistic approach, whatever we do. One idea is to blitz the market with advertising to motivate the best prospects—the low hanging fruit—to attend the boat show in the first place."*

Susan (industry consultant): *"That's a great idea, Abbud. Building on that, one idea to consider that's worked in other spaces is a kind of a guerrilla marketing campaign where we use our market optimization algorithm to create heat maps identifying Census tracks with the highest market potential. Before the boat show, we drop off a specially designed packet door-to-door talking about the benefits of boating to these prospective first-timers."*

Jerry: *"Yes, we need to do a paradigm shift in the minds of these prospects."*

Definition: An *Argument by Gibberish* is one in which the use of trivial, unintelligible language and jargon make the argument's conclusion appear to be sound. In the previous example, the conclusion is that targeting first-time boat buyers will help expand the market and, presumably, Apollo's sales. The conclusion may seem plausible to some because this strategy involves "blitzing" the market, incorporating a "guerrilla marketing campaign" that is guided by an "optimization algorithm" to attract the "low hanging fruit." The marketing communications will result in a "paradigm shift" in prospects' minds. The strategy should work because it has worked in "other spaces." All this, of course, is hogwash—although the preceding vignette is drawn from an actual experience!

Discussion

We all are guilty of using Argument by Gibberish at least sometimes because it often works as shorthand for a longer thought. For instance, "other spaces" is short for "other nonboating markets." "Low hanging fruit" is short for "targeting prospects that are most likely to consider a brand," and "paradigm shift" is short for "changing how target prospects think about boating."

The use of gibberish is rife in the marketing industry, especially in popular marketing books and conferences. Keep in mind that all marketing books and conference presentations are really arguments, and their conclusions are along the lines of "therefore ... use our method, do X in this way, hire me," and so on. For instance, while writing this book, we received several marketing conference brochures and e-mail notices that included the following examples.

... to maximize personal connections	The solution is a digital engagement strategy	... [offering] a seamless experience.
... digital engagement implementation	... optimizing operational structures	... data fusion linking purchasing, on-line activity ....
... create interactive visualizations	... right-size [your] approach to data analytics	A/B experiments are a great point-of-entry ....
... gives us a 3D digital shopper engine	... omnichannel marketing scorecard design	... reverse engineering ....
... harmonize brand-building metrics	... data intelligence [that expresses] itself with its own personality and voice.	... distilling the digital into the personal.

The use of gibberish to help support an argument reflects muddled thinking and should raise a red flag—does the person using Argument by Gibberish really know what he is talking about? One of the consultants who participated in the meeting on which the aforementioned vignette is based suggested a "guerrilla marketing strategy" targeting current boat owners in which marketing communication packets would be surreptitiously placed on high-end boats (presumably in the early morning hours when everyone was asleep) docked at affluent marinas. What the consultant did not know is that these marinas are secured so that only boat owners and their families have access to them. Guerrilla marketers—STAY AWAY!

Dealing with Argument by Gibberish

There is really only one way to deal with this logical fallacy—have the person making an Argument by Gibberish clarify his terms. Then, once you understand what is meant by the term, explore how that term helps support the person's conclusion.

This can be difficult if the person basing an Argument by Gibberish really does not know what he's talking about. In the business meeting on which this fallacy's vignette is based, both the CMO and consultants were making so many arguments by gibberish that any attempt to have them clarify what they meant would have ground the meeting to a halt and greatly irritated the CMO.

Argument to Moderation

Location: Quarterly production planning meeting in a consumer durables company.

Issue: Attendees are presenting and discussing product sales forecasts and production capacity to arrive at the next quarter's production plan.

> Tom (brand manager): *"Our forecast is to sell 120,000 units next quarter."*
>
> Bill (plant manager): *"I think that's overly optimistic, Tom. Based on our review of past plant production, I think we'll be lucky to hit 80,000 units. We have 20,000 units in inventory, and our plant can produce 40,000— that gives us 60,000. So it looks like we are going to be short 20,000 units by my reckoning, but 60,000 by yours."*
>
> John (marketing director): *"Historically, neither of you have been very accurate in your forecasts. Brand people tend to be too optimistic and plant managers too pessimistic. So let's split the difference between 120,000 and 80,000 and assume that sales are going to be 100,000 units. If we have 20,000 units in inventory, and we can produce 40,000, that gives us 60,000 units. We'll be 'short' by 40,000 units. Bill, you figure out how we can make up the difference and, Tom, drop your forecast by 20,000."*

Compromise is necessary in business right? Not when it comes to the truth. In the aforementioned case, if the plant capacity or the sales forecasts have not been "padded" or "sandbagged," then a compromise could lead to a disaster hurting both parties.

Definition: An *Argument to Moderation* (also called "splitting the difference") occurs when one asserts that the midpoint between two opposing propositions is true (or more likely to be true) without providing any evidence supporting that assertion.

Discussion

Research on this logical fallacy finds that some sources assume that the two opposing propositions must be extremes on a continuum. Others don't make this assumption. In our previous example, the marketing director states that, historically, brand management's forecasts have been too optimistic and plant management's too pessimistic, which reflects two extremes on a continuum.

Actual sales may indeed "fall in the middle." But what makes the marketing director's "compromise" an Argument to Moderation is that *he gives no evidence to support it.* Historically, brand may *tend* to be optimistic, and the plant may *tend* to be pessimistic, but that does not mean that their forecasts are always wrong. If one of them is right this time, "splitting the difference" could precipitate a disaster.

If the plant's capacity were in fact 40,000 units per quarter and actual sales were indeed 120,000 units, John is trying to force a compromise that will ultimately make both Bill and Tom's staffs look bad. Worst case, it may set off a chain reaction in which forecasts are artificially inflated so that "there is always enough to sell," and the plant's capacity is expanded to meet them. The end result is dead inventory and a plant running under capacity. Hard to believe? We've seen it happen and maybe you have too.

Dealing with Argument to Moderation

If you are in a marketing setting where compromise is proposed, ask a few questions (perhaps to yourself at first) to determine if the proposed compromise is an Argument to Moderation:

1. Can the compromise position really be achieved by all parties involved? Really?
2. What evidence supports the compromise as being closer to the truth than the opposing propositions?
3. Is either of the positions *capable* of any middle ground?
4. What would be the outcome of a failed compromise? How would this affect the organization?
5. What would happen if no compromise were achieved? Assess the impact of either or both of the two positions being played out to their completion.

Compromise may be the best outcome in some marketing situations, but not all. Choose this solution carefully to make sure that the outcome isn't worse than either of the alternatives.

Sometimes the middle ground can run you off the road.

Biased Sample

Location: Product launch planning meeting in a medical products company.

Issue: Managers are discussing product packaging for a new eye drop in preparation for the product's introduction.

> Terry (product manager): *"I am really pleased with the results of the packaging research we conducted; it clearly shows that the packaging we chose meets the customer's needs and is at least as good as our leading competitor."*
>
> Mark (VP marketing): *"Wait, I was at the interviews in Boston, and that is not what they said at all. I clearly remember that one guy who thought our packaging was too hard to open and squeeze. I think we have to go back to the drawing board and rethink the packaging."*
>
> Shelly (market research manager): *"Mark, although there were a few Boston respondents who didn't care for our packaging, we did 100 interviews across 10 cities, and over 80% of respondents preferred our package to our competitors'."*
>
> Mark: *"I just can't believe that—I saw it with my own eyes in Boston. I've said all along—our packaging is not going to get the job done."*

Shelly and Terry were just on the receiving end of a biased sample. Mark has chosen to use the sample (the few interviews he saw) that he believes to be relevant to the decision, instead of the entire sample included in the study. Unless they can get Mark to believe in the totality of the research, it's going to be a long meeting.

Definition: The *Biased Sample* occurs when a conclusion is made based on a research sample that is biased in some way, or from a sample selected in such a way that it does not truly represent the population from which it was taken (i.e., a nonrepresentative sample). When this happens, you expose yourself to a situation in which the information you are collecting from the sample may be biased as well. You might luck out—biased samples can sometimes generate unbiased information—but don't count on it. You're better off in the long run collecting samples that have the least amount of bias possible.

Discussion

Conclusions that result from biased samples are all around us. They are often prefaced by the words, "Studies show that ..." or "Research has shown that ...." Be wary of statistics (especially in an election year), as they can be used to inappropriately validate conclusions.

Marketing conclusions that arise as a result of biased samples usually don't carry the seemingly ominous intent of those that occur in politics, but can be hugely damaging to the success of products and organizations. Some common examples of problems that result from biased samples in marketing are:

- Failing to select or weigh data to reflect the population as a whole, versus just using the raw data for your analysis. For example, we often have to reweigh survey data to reflect the age of the customer base as a whole, rather than just those who actually completed the survey.
- Drawing the sample from too selective of a pool of respondents, for example, limiting a survey to households of four or more, even when the product will also be marketed to two-person households.
- Assuming that consumers from different ethnic groups will behave in a manner that is the same as the "random sample."
- Assuming that a "large" survey (say 1,000 consumers) is accurate just because it is large, regardless of other criteria that may indicate those 1,000 people may not adequately represent the potential population of 100 million.

- Ignoring known (or suspected) regional differences in behavior when surveying respondents.
- "Loading" a sample with customers who are advocates of your company or product (or at least not controlling for this).

Dealing with Biased Sample

As Mark Twain often said, there are "Lies, damned lies, and statistics." As a first step, be sure that you, as a marketer, are using statistics in a valid way by ensuring that your data are as unbiased as possible. If you are uncertain, consult your company's marketing research professionals or get advice from outside research consultants.

When faced with what you feel may be biased samples, ask yourself (and your coworkers) the following questions:

1. Is the sample we are basing the decision on (or preparing to gather insight from) fully and completely representative of the population we are trying to reach?
2. Have we designed the sample to adequately address any hypotheses that we need to test (e.g., different hypotheses may relate to different populations of consumers)?
3. Does the person or group supporting the "biased" data have a reason for that bias?

What can the managers in our example do to address Mark's concerns? Stick to the facts. Try to show the VP that customers as a whole support the new packaging as is. Remember, only ask questions you *really* want the answers to.

Causal Oversimplification

Location: Agricultural chemical marketing "war room."

Issue: Sales and marketing teams are discussing the causes of a sales decline in the company's Capital brand herbicide that is used with GMO—genetically modified organism—seed corn. (For our nonagricultural readers:

many herbicides today that control for weeds and grasses are marketed in tandem with GMO seed, where the herbicide kills all plants except the crop itself, such as corn or soybeans.)

Randy (marketing manager): *"I've heard that farmers are complaining about Capital's effect on corn yields. What are you hearing, Jack?"*

Jack (sales manager): *"Same thing. I was in Iowa just last week talking to about 10 farmers and some of our distributors. They are all talking about yield. Capital is not strong enough on waterhemp and Palmer's pigweed, and that apparently is causing some yield loss in the corn."*

Gene (marketing research manager): *"Our research points to the same conclusion; however, this may be being caused by some other factors, like the farmer diluting the herbicide too much to save money."*

Randy: *"Farmers may be cheap, but they're not stupid, Gene. Capital just isn't strong enough to control some weeds—we need to spike it with another chemical."*

Randy is focusing on a single cause of the herbicide's poor performance. In reality, few marketing outcomes are the result of a single factor.

Definition: *Causal Oversimplification,* sometimes called "causal reductionism," assumes that a single cause can explain a particular effect.

Discussion

There are other logical fallacies—for example, Argument to Moderation and Affirming the Consequent—that focus directly or indirectly on misunderstanding cause and effect relationships. Causal Oversimplification is yet another fallacious way of thinking that often gets the relationships between causes and their effects wrong.

Marketing is one area in which a single factor will rarely explain any outcome. In part, this is because products or services are supported by a "marketing mix" (the good old 4P's: product, price, place, and promotion). Marketing mix variables such as the quality and extent of advertising, being priced competitively, and having adequate distribution and channel support, all can affect a product's success or failure. Additional factors may relate to competitors' product offerings; in the case of herbicide performance, the weather plays a huge role, and those involved in that business know this. Additionally, herbicide performance can be affected by "application timing"—applying the product too early or too late in the growing season can affect herbicide performance and resultant crop yields.

In the earlier vignette, Randy is prone to attribute a single cause— poor weed and grass control—to Capital's sales decline. And his solution is just as single-minded—spike Capital with chemicals that will control for waterhemp and pigweed and not harm the crop. In reality, there are usually several alternative actions that should be considered. By oversimplifying both the problem and the solution, it may appear to some that Randy is running his own agenda or is "on a mission" for some reason. In doing this, he may be inadvertently setting himself up to be viewed, not as a "problem solver," but as someone who is out for himself.

In reality (this vignette is based on an actual example), the cause of Capital's sales decline was related to *many* factors, such as farmers using a weak concentration of Capital in their sprayer, product contamination with another herbicide that was used in the same sprayer that Capital was used in, and improper application of the herbicide on the corn crop.

Of course there may be situations in which a single cause can explain most or all of a marketing outcome. Colgate Kitchen Entrées is one example: The brand name of this marketing failure was simply incongruent with the product.[11]

Dealing with Causal Oversimplification

A very useful strategy in addressing this fallacy is contained in the Think Better piece, "The 5 Whys." Gene and Jack might have asked Randy why he thinks Capital herbicide was producing such poor yields. The first "why" might have been answered with, "Because it can't control waterhemp and pigweed," but the subsequent "whys" would have helped Gene to make his case—if only to gain consensus for conducting a marketing research study to explore the issue in greater depth.

Experienced teams (or teams with experienced people) usually have less difficulty in handling this fallacy; they simply do what they should do—"root around" to look for more than one cause of a complex problem.

Inexperience can lead to knee-jerk decisions when a plausible solution is put forward. It's easy to rally behind the solution because no one has adequate scar tissue to challenge it. Leaders and team members in this situation must be careful not to jump to conclusions.

Paraphrasing H.L. Menken, complex questions have simple, easy-to-understand answers that are usually wrong.

Conflict of Interest

Location: Annual sales goal-setting meeting for a major auto parts manufacturer.

Issue: Regional sales managers are negotiating annual sales goals with their boss, the national sales manager. Also present is the VP of marketing.

Duane (western regional sales manager): *"I just don't see how we can plan for more than $1 million from Acme Distributing next year. They will do $1 million with us this year, but I sense we are really topped out there."*

Bob (national sales manager): *"I agree with you Duane. Counting on Acme for more than $1 million next year is too big a stretch. Let's put them down for $900,000."*

Alan (VP of marketing): *"So this is how it goes, huh? You guys just sit around and guess how much you are going to sell next year so that your bonuses are comfortable. Well, the rest of us are setting stretch goals, and I don't like it that you guys are sandbagging."*

Bob: *"That's not at all what is happening, and I really don't like you insinuating that we are up to something devious. We want the company to be successful, and these numbers are our best estimates."*

Definition: A *Conflict of Interest* occurs when someone suggests that another person's (or group's) argument is invalid, not because of any factual reasons, but because the person making the argument is biased. This is a relative of the personal attack fallacy known as "Ad Hominem" and is also referred to as "questioning motives" or "having a vested interest."

Discussion

Alan jumped to a very general conclusion that the sales managers were sandbagging their budgets to ensure that their earnings were secure. This may or may not have been the case.

There are many reasons why Alan arrived at this conclusion. For example, he may have been "profiling" the sales managers, using old stereotypes of "how salespeople act" as the basis for his conclusion. Whatever the reason, Alan's open assertion that the sales managers were acting in a self-serving manner likely ground the meeting to a stop, ending the "open sharing" between participants.

But what if Alan had only raised these concerns "in his head," rather than speaking them outright? An interpersonal "explosion" might have been avoided in the meeting, but problems would likely still linger to threaten the organization. Being skeptical of the "sandbagged" budget, Alan might fail to support it with upper management or make side comments to the chief financial officer (CFO).

However, what if the sales budget was indeed being sandbagged? If that were the case and no one "called" the sales management team on it, the end result could be big sales bonuses, but also inaccurate forecasting, inventory shortages, and a healthy dose of finger pointing and bad feelings after the fact.

Conflict of Interest is not at all limited to interactions with coworkers. Think of your interactions over the years with vendors, customers, or even outside parties like regulatory agencies. You may find situations where an assumed conflict reared its head. If handled improperly, the ramifications can be huge—lost customers, fractured vendor relationships, and added costs.

Dealing with Conflict of Interest

So what to do? In our previous case, there clearly should be some middle ground—a way to challenge the sales budget without making a personal attack. In our experience, dealing with Conflict of Interest requires deft interpersonal skills. Some suggestions:

1. Don't resort to discipline "stereotypes" (e.g., sales is always out to sandbag its budgets).
2. Choose your words carefully. In the sales budgeting meeting, the company would have been better served if Alan had not directly "called out" Duane, but rather challenged him in a more tactful manner.
3. Ask more questions to clarify the situation and bring the discussion back to facts and data. Alan could have asked a series of questions directed at understanding the details of how the sales budget was created.
4. Work to fix systems that drive conflict. In this case, don't let salespeople set their sales targets or, better yet, don't let people design their own pay no matter what department (a correction which has not made it to all boardrooms yet).
5. Find a second layer of measures that helps protect against conflicts. For example, in the aforementioned case, the issue could be mitigated by adding a forecast accuracy measure to the compensation equation.

Finally, if you feel that others may perceive *you* to be the one with a conflict of interest, face it head on, and soon. Acknowledge the potential conflict up front and then explain why you are either not conflicted or how you are dealing with the situation.

Was the sales budget sandbagged? We'll never know, but it is safe to assume that Alan did not receive a guest invitation to the year-end sales incentive trip.

Counterfactual Fallacy

Location: Pet food manufacturer's "offsite" marketing meeting.

Issue: The market's lukewarm reception to the company's new cat-food brand brings together the marketing and sales team to discuss what caused this disappointing launch and what can be done about it.

Shelly (VP sales): *"We have not met our quarterly projections for nearly 18 months. The sales team attributes this to the manufacturing delays at our Milwaukee plant that resulted in half of our distribution* [pet-food retailers] *not getting their initial orders. So half the money we spent on marketing support was wasted."*

David (VP marketing): *"It's a fact that manufacturing dropped the ball. But you'll recall that, at the time of market launch, the company cut our sales force by 10% in order to 'make the numbers' for headquarters. If we had kept our sales force intact, then we would not be where we are today. They could have compensated for the initial trip up in manufacturing."*

David is making an appeal to the "counterfactual" because his argument is based on a hypothetical claim—keeping the sales force in place would have compensated for the company's manufacturing problems at the time of product launch.

Definition: The *Counterfactual Fallacy*, sometimes referred to as the "hypothesis contrary to fact," is an error of reasoning in which what might have occurred in the past or will occur in the future would have led or will lead to some stated outcome supporting an argument and, often, criticizing the soundness of someone else's.

Discussion

A counterfactual statement is presented in opposition to a stated fact. Often this stated fact is the premise of another argument. Shelly states the fact that manufacturing was unable to keep up with retail orders of the new product. No one disputes this—it's a fact. However, David makes the counterfactual claim that *if* the sales force had not been cut, *then* the new product launch would have been successful, without presenting any evidence to back up his argument.

The Counterfactual Fallacy often is a cousin to Causal Oversimplification, a fallacy in which one or a few factors are attributed to the cause of a complex event. Generally, the world is more complicated than that implied by the use of these two fallacies. As the logical fallacy blogger, Norm Jenson, says about the Counterfactual Fallacy:

"In a complex situation, other factors [in addition to the counterfactual claim] are likely to intervene. The boundary between clear situations and

complex situations is, of course, broad and fuzzy, and the fuzziness of the boundary allows fallacious reasoning to masquerade as good practical speculation. The connection between failing to turn in assignments and failing to pass ... [a] class is simple and obvious. It is easy to understand how things would have turned out differently if the assignments had been turned in. The connection between [for example] gun ownership and levels of crime in a community are complex and indirect. In that context we can't easily project how things would be different if circumstances were changed. Nevertheless, our usual success with speculative reasoning (in simpler contexts) may embolden us into thinking that we can speculate successfully even here."[12]

Dealing with the Counterfactual Fallacy

Counterfactual statements are speculative and often hard to support with evidence. This is because they make false claims about a historical or future situation. Because of this, the easiest way to support a counterfactual claim so that it does not become a fallacy of reasoning is to make an appeal to a similar situation—citing relevant past events as analogies. For example, David may have identified a historical event where the sales force in fact did compensate for a shortage of supply because of manufacturing problems and maintained the growth projection of another company product. In short, *find strong analogies* that support a counterfactual statement.

If you had purchased this book a year earlier, *then* you'd be twice as successful as you are today!

"E" for Effort

Location: Quarterly review of Marketing Talent Development Program projects.

Issue: Do our product naming conventions need updating? Han, a middle manager, is a leadership talent development candidate. His manager, Leia, serves as Han's "sponsor" or mentor in this program.

Han (marketing leadership talent development candidate): *"I sent out a Survey Monkey questionnaire to 742 of our employees asking them to rate several aspects of our historical product naming conventions and to compare those evaluations against using more colorful and descriptive names. I received 62 responses: 52 from engineering, 8 from operations and 2 from sales."*

Darth (sales leader): *"Did you ask any customers?"*

Han: *"No."*

Leia: (Han's sponsor): *"We thought the research like this might be too confidential. If customers knew what we were up to, our competitors would quickly find out. Changing our product nomenclature strategy would be a big change for us. So we surveyed more people and did more analysis."*

Han: *"As you can see in these 12 survey results charts, no matter how you slice it or control for the different questions, the conclusion is that we should keep our current product naming conventions."*

Leia: *"Very nice charts Han. Also I would like to add that you can't see how extensive the spread sheets are that Han put together to analyze the survey results. He really put a lot of work into the analysis and knows his Excel Pivot Tables. Thank you for that great review of your work. Who is next?"*

Wait! Is no one going to skewer this? Han did a lot of work, so are we just going to give him an "E" for effort in our Leadership Talent Development Program, or are we going to demand sound results?

Definition: We fall into the *"E" for Effort* trap when we are too polite and accept a conclusion because of the notable effort invested, even if it is unrelated to the truth or fails to advance our thinking.

Discussion

Let us remember, E is between D and F—not a good enough grade to pass, let alone win awards. This kind of logical fallacy can creep into our thinking when we want to be nice more than we want to be right. It is especially easy to fall into this trap when we have a high degree of apathy for the subject at hand and it's easier to collect the political brownie points than it is to be right all the time (maybe in the aforementioned scene, Darth gives Leia a knowing glance that says, *"This work stinks; you owe me one for not calling you out."*).

Dealing with "E" for Effort

Those of us who think marketing is actually just as much a science as it is an art need to protect our profession against too much "E" for Effort logic. It devalues the discipline. And there is nothing less disciplined than an "E" for Effort mentality or the unwillingness to call it out, even in public settings.

Yes, there are times when it is better to let these things lie and pick your battles. But if you notice that your marketing organization is letting things lie more often than it is showing the discipline to demand good marketing science then you need to raise alarms. We can't accept notable effort in place of sound results.

In some companies, it is hard for marketing to achieve the same level of "importance" as finance, engineering, or operations possess. These are disciplines that no one disputes are methodical, and they're "older" functions as well. So, it's imperative for those in marketing to be extra-methodical and extra-disciplined to fight for and keep a seat at the big-boys' table. If your marketing organization is seen as one that values effort over results (input over output), then you will understand when you are not asked to weigh in on the important decisions.

Thinking of marketing as a science can combat "E" for Effort. Look at the results of a market analysis or research study and determine if they were conclusive and valuable. Also, examine the soundness of the methods (quality of and difficulty of methods are not causally linked): Are they capable and current? If you cannot answer "yes" to all of these, then speak up, ask questions. This is the best way to be the least offensive but also show that, while the wheels were spinning, the car didn't move. "How many customers did you talk to?" "Did you compare this to academic practices?" "What does current academic or third-party research suggest?"

False Dilemma

Location: A high-performance team outing for the leadership team on a high-ropes course. Note: "A *ropes course* is a challenging outdoor personal development and team building activity which usually consists of high or low elements. *Low elements* take place on the ground or only a few feet above the ground. *High elements* are usually constructed in trees or made of utility poles and require abelay for safety."[13]

Issue: Modernizing the channel.

> Stikinda (VP of accounting): *"Look, we are either all in or all out. My team cannot support the dealer channel, as we do today, and your risky e-commerce strategy as well."*

> Bluusi (VP of marketing): *"It is not a risky strategy. It's only that it won't work well for the latest high-touch, customized products. I wouldn't think of putting them online."*

> Stikinda: *"Our dealers will surely revolt. Our only choice is to keep all our lines in our full-line, full-service dealer network or pull it all out and go online with everything, which you said won't work with the high-touch customized products."*

So Stikinda wants to stay the course and Bluusi wants to try new things. But it's not the fact that Stikinda is conservative that makes him the antagonist, or that Bluusi is creative which makes her the protagonist. It is that Stikinda is arguing from extremes, presenting limited and false alternatives.

Definition: A *False Dilemma* is created when typically two (but there could be three or more) alternatives are presented as the sole alternatives when, actually, there are more possible alternatives (explanations, choices, etc.) that have been omitted, either erroneously or purposefully. Usually the presented alternatives are extremes designed to make a choice seem cut and dried.

Discussion

Business at its root is about making better (more profitable) decisions than the competition. Usually marketing should play a major role in the business decision-making process. Typically we think of marketing decisions in the classical 4P's domains: What *product* should we make? How should we *price* it? How should we *promote* it so it takes the greatest market share? And where should we *place* it to sell best? These key business decisions often are presented as discrete options. It is far too complex to get an organization to make a decision when the options are collectively exhaustive or, even worse, a continuum of infinite options. So we usually resort to discrete cases pitted against each other.

Dealing with False Dilemma

The solution to this fallacy is easy: Explore more alternatives. You must open people's minds to the fact that other alternatives exist. You could try to sound very executive-like:

> *"When I was at McKinsey and Co., we saw the need to be more MECE before we started narrowing our options. Oh, you poor ignorant accountant, you are not schooled in consultant-speak? That's Mutually Exclusive and Collectively Exhaustive. We need to get MECE before we gravitate to any false alternatives. Now pass me some of those chocolates, I'm starving."*

Or you could do something pragmatic like propose to find something in the middle and test it—even if only qualitatively at first. Then, as always, back the options up as much as you can with some good research, data, and analysis (in that order).

> *"Stikinda, you're presenting two extreme alternatives. It's false logic to think we are stuck in such a dilemma. What I think I will do when I get back to the office is call one or two of my favorite dealers and see if they would consider an alternative where we move the commodity products online and out of their stores and replace them with the new line which has more margin for them and for us. This would give them the shelf space they need without having to invest capital. I think they will see this as a win."*

False Precision

Location: Corporate board room of a national consumer packaged-goods company.

Situation: A marketing research firm is presenting the results of a product concept study that was commissioned by the company. The research firm tested several shelf-stable entrée items (i.e., frozen meals you can heat and eat out of a box).

> Geoffrey (marketing research consultant): *"The study's sample size was 1,500 completed interviews conducted via a national representative panel of target consumers. Product Concept D received the highest overall rating of 8.763 on our 10-point scale, where higher numbers denote better perceived performance of the concept on the rated attributes."*

> Mary (product manager): *"Both the sample size and the average rating are impressive. I'm amazed at the high level of precision you've incorporated into this study."*

On what basis does Mary attribute the characteristic of "precision" to this study? We suspect it is because of the relatively large sample size and the fact that the mean attribute scores are presented to the third decimal place.

Definition: *False Precision* occurs when one uses data to falsely or artificially strengthen the premises of an argument, suggesting that the argument is more valid than it truly is.

Discussion

In the marketing world, one of the most fertile fields in which one may find the False Precision fallacy is marketing research. But these fallacies can crop up in any analysis that involves statistics, such as quality control:

> *"Our findings are based on examining 400 products coming off the production floor, and we only identified manufacturing flaws in 2.677 percent of the products."*

Or you can sometimes find this fallacy in competitive intelligence reports:

> *"Using text analytics software, and scouring over 10,000 printed sources, we found only 10 references to the new technology."*

The statistics in these examples suggest that a high level of analytical precision was undertaken by the analysts because of the studies' large sample sizes and statistical estimates. Precision is a comforting concept to audiences on the receiving end of reports and presentations. Statistics that suggest highly thorough methods and analysis give the impression of being "precise," "scientific," "accurate," when they actually might not be—creating a false sense of security that the information can be trusted. False Precision often clothes unscientific methods and inaccurate results in very attractive, multicolored, and sometimes multimedia Power Point presentations.

In the quality control example, the reported flaw rate of 2.677 percent can actually be off by as much as 1.7 percentage points, given the sample size of 400 (at the 95 percent level of confidence). The statistic 2.677 has no statistical significance at the second decimal place!

Scouring 10,000 articles in the competitive intelligence study can produce extremely biased results if the search was not based on a representative sample of publications read by the relevant population of interest. And since two of the authors of this book are professional marketing researchers, we can tell you to be highly suspicious of any research firm reporting attribute ratings to the second or third decimal place. Research study sample sizes rarely are large enough to produce mean estimates of attribute ratings that are statistically significant beyond the first decimal place.

Keep these definitions in mind when reviewing statistical claims: "Accuracy" is *validity*. A statistic's accuracy reflects how close to the truth the statistic is. "Precision" is *reliable repeatability*. If you were to repeat the same study, would you get the same answer, within the margin of statistical sampling error? These two terms are often used interchangeably, but each has a different meaning.

A statistic may be "precise," but not be "accurate" if it is based on a biased sample. For example, in our experience, many Internet-based consumer surveys generally under sample nonwhite populations or students in college. This may or may not lead to biased answers to survey questions, but it could if nonwhite and student population behaviors and attitudes differed from other target population members. In B2B studies, not interviewing a representative sample of decision makers or the actual decision makers can result in a biased sample and, likely, biased answers to your questions.

Dealing with False Precision

You don't need a degree in statistics or marketing research to deal with this fallacy effectively. Here are some questions you might ask those who are producing the statistics to help you differentiate *precise* statistics from *accurate* ones:

- For this statistic, what is the sampling error? Larger sample sizes produce smaller levels of sampling error.
- For this statistic, how appropriate is it to take this number to the first decimal place, second decimal place (insert the appropriate term, based on whether the statistic is a percentage, dollar amount, or something else)?
- What potential biases might be inherent in the sample from which this statistic is based? How might those biases affect the accuracy or validity of the statistic?
- How might the wording of the question on which this statistic is based affect the statistic's validity? For example, simply asking people an open-ended question about what brand of refrigerator they own will provide a different answer than asking respondents to first check the name of their refrigerator brand in their kitchen and then report it.

Here's a simple way to imagine the concepts of accuracy versus precision Figure 5.1:

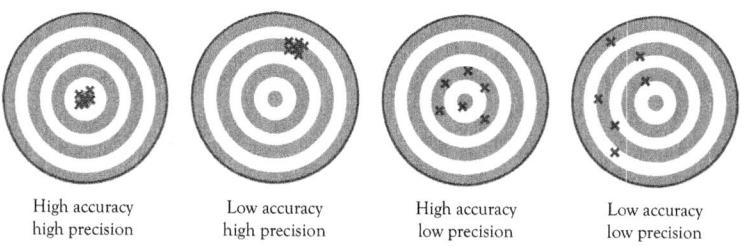

| High accuracy | Low accuracy | High accuracy | Low accuracy |
| high precision | high precision | low precision | low precision |

Figure 5.1 Accuracy versus precision

Faulty Comparison

Location: A marketing conference room.

Issue: A marketing research manager and a product manager are reviewing proposals to conduct a marketing research study on a new product.

Akio (product manager): *"Thanks for working with all the research suppliers to get these bids. I've reviewed them, and it looks to me like we get more for our money if we go with Acme Research. Their cost-per-interview for the qualitative research is $500, and their cost-per-interview for the follow-up quantitative study is $150. These prices are at least 20% less than the other bids we received."*

David (marketing research manager): *"Yes, that's correct; however, the analysts from Market Insights Company have more experience. Those who will be conducting the exploratory research interviews each have over 25 years' experience conducting qualitative interviews in our product category. The Acme interviewers have, at most, three years' experience in the category. Also, Market Insights is recommending a more advanced statistical analysis of the data than is Acme. In the long run, I think we are more likely to make a better decision if we go with Market Insights."*

Akio: *"But Market Insights costs more for the same number of interviews!!"*

Akio is using a "faulty comparison" to support his recommendation to use Acme Research. David thinks he's comparing "apples to oranges."

Definition: A *Faulty Comparison* is a fallacy in which two things are compared in an incomplete way to make one appear more or less desirable than another. Akio is only comparing the proposals on price—an incomplete comparison. He then infers that because Acme's proposal is the least expensive, his department would get more value from that firm. This is like saying that, because cauliflower and chocolate bars are both snacks, you should always eat chocolate because it tastes better.

Discussion

Comparing "apples to oranges" is an invalid comparison. In the previous example, Akio's argument contains the presupposition that the Acme and

Market Insights proposals share similar properties, except one—cost. David points out to him that there are other properties in which the proposals differ, namely the level of experience of the qualitative interviewers and the level of statistical analysis in the quantitative portion of the research. This situation is, unfortunately, all too common in marketing research when bids are reduced to a "cost-per-complete" and everything else is assumed to be "equal."

We often encounter faulty comparisons in advertising. For example, in 2007, the Evinrude division of Bombardier Recreational Products put out a video advertisement via the Internet and a DVD through its retail distributors comparing its 150 HP outboard engine to Mercury Marine's 150 HP outboard engine. This was a faulty comparison because the Evinrude's lighter, two-stroke engine was being compared to Mercury's heavier four-stroke engine. The ratio of engine power to engine weight can have a significant effect on engine performance—for example, faster speed and faster acceleration in the case of the lighter Evinrude engine. At the time, Mercury did not have a 150 HP two-stroke engine, yet Evinrude used the faulty comparison to promote its product.

Sometimes faulty comparisons can creep into marketing strategies. *"If we want to increase sales, let's increase spending on digital advertising versus magazine advertising—the cost-per-exposure is cheaper for digital."* This argument is, once again, comparing apples to oranges because it makes digital and magazine advertising share similar properties except cost. The comparison between the two media is incomplete and misleading because they can differ on many other properties, such as average exposure time, size of the advertisement, and amount of information contained in the ad.

Dealing with Faulty Comparison

When confronted with a possible faulty comparison, assess it on two factors: relevance and significance. Are the objects being compared on attributes that are relevant to the argument, and are the objects significantly the same or different on these attributes to make for a persuasive comparison in supporting an argument?

In the aforementioned vignette, Akio tacitly assumes that the quality of the proposals is the same. The only relevant difference he sees is price.

Akio did not think of comparing the proposals (or purposely chose not to?) on other relevant attributes such as the quality of the interviewers or the statistical analysis. So, in examining a potential faulty comparison analogy, ask yourself, *"Are we comparing X and Y on all relevant attributes, or just on those that support the proponent's conclusion?"*

Whenever someone uses an analogy to support an argument, a red light should go off in your head. Analogies or comparisons are rarely perfect. And, if someone is using a comparison to persuade you to take one action over another, ponder the quality of the analogy carefully. Start by listing other relevant and significant attributes that should be considered and suggest that the group explore them. Apples and oranges may both be fruit, but if you want apple juice, don't squeeze an orange.

Generalization

Location: Dealer visit.

Issue: How much inventory should the dealer carry?

Scott (dealer sales executive): *"You should always carry more inventory of everything if you want to grow your sales. Tom, you can't sell from an empty shelf. If the basket is empty, nobody buys."*

Tom (dealer principal): *"No way Scott. It's too risky. Plus, you're over-simplifying just to get an order and hit your numbers. Then you'll walk out quickly to the next dealer. Does your inventory rule always apply? Does it trump good decision-making? I can think of a lot of exceptions to your 'rule': perishable products, products with fast developing technologies, seasonal products, 'fashion-forward' or trendy products, and products that customers expect or even want to wait for, like a custom motorcycle, a product I can drop ship and still meet delivery expectations. No. I think we should always carry inventory ONLY on those products that have a high turnover. So you can either walk out now without my order, or we can sit down and try to find a decision-making strategy that is not a fallacy."*

Definition: When a rule is overused, it can become a *Generalization Fallacy*. Sometimes the rule doesn't fit because of an overwhelming number of exceptions: "A" is always true. Except in cases where B, or C, or D, or E, or F, or G, or H, or I, or J, ... or X. So, basically, the argument is that "A" is always true with a set of conditions that rarely or never exists. So is it really "always true?"

Discussion

Generalizations are often used in arguments. They are sometimes part of a good set of assumptions or rules of thumb. But, as we know from other discussions in this book, if an argument is dependent on other conditions, we should check to make sure those conditions are, in fact, correct. In the case of the fallacy, one's logic is faulty when an argument sounds good or a generalization is asserted that sounds simple, except for a large number of stated or unstated exceptions or conditions.

Dealing with the Generalization Fallacy

Are there lots of caveats? Become suspicious. The assertion may sound simple and enticing but, if it has a large number of exceptions, then the likelihood is that it is not true.

Like so many other logical fallacies, the remedy is simply to ask repeated layers of questions, such as The 5 Whys (see Think Better: The 5 Whys), or to go searching for solid links back to a cause and effect: *"Are you sure this applies? But what about_____? "And none of those exceptions matter in this case?" "Simple logic but is this the simple case?"*

Guilt by Association

Location: Company cafeteria of a pharmaceutical manufacturer at lunchtime, during the middle of the annual budget cycle.

Issue: R&D project managers are discussing presentation plans that soon will be made to upper management. They notice that two of their peers, Dan and Sharon (who were invited to this lunch meeting but declined), are having a private lunch with Jim, the head of R&D, at a table across the courtyard.

Susan (project manager 1): *"Looks like Dan and Sharon found a better date for lunch. Wonder what they are talking about?"*

Richard (project manager 2): *"Like you can't guess. Sharon is doing her usual end-run on the budgeting process with Jim. Happens every year."*

Terry (project manager 3): *"She knows how to work the system. She is so competitive about getting her projects funded that I really do not like her as a team member. I find that I just don't share anything with her anymore because it comes back to haunt me."*

Susan: *"What surprises me is that Dan is in there too—I didn't expect that behavior from him. Guess I'm going to have to be careful about what I share with him too."*

Richard: *"Looks like we all may have to be more careful."*

Definition: *Guilt by Association* occurs when someone is viewed negatively because of his association with someone else who is viewed negatively. In this case, Dan is guilty by association with Sharon, who has a reputation of getting her way in the budgeting process at the expense of other project managers. This is another example of the personal-attack fallacy known as "Ad Hominem"—also referred to as the "company you keep" or "bad company" fallacy.

Discussion

"I don't like that crowd you are hanging around with. They are going to get you into trouble." Probably everyone has heard a version of this from his or her parents in adolescence. Many of us who have become parents have completed the circle by speaking (or at least thinking) a version of the same advice to our children. Like it or not, the "company you keep" often has an impact on how you are perceived in the world. Hang with the "cool kids" often enough and you become perceived as one. Hang with the nerds and, well, you get the idea. (Spoiler alert—none of the authors was in the cool group. Go figure.)

In the marketing world, the same can be true. Associating with persons, beliefs, or causes that are perceived negatively "rubs off" on you—right or wrong.

Guilt by Association is not limited to people—"things" (ideas, concepts, methods, etc.) also can be labeled unfairly as "bad" by being associated with other negatively perceived things. Think about marketing projects you may have been involved in that were branded "unworthy" simply because of their similarity to or association with other projects that "failed."

Guilt by Association can also work in reverse as well, in which case it might be called "The Coattails Fallacy." A successful marketing program does not mean that all the elements in a marketing program were good ones.

Dealing with Guilt by Association

Disciplined, logical, scientific marketing professionals should not validate Guilt by Association. Avoid this fallacy by doing the following:

- Get the facts, and don't jump to conclusions.
- Take some time to study the situation to determine if the person (or thing) in question is really guilty of some objectionable behavior or just "bad company."
- Ask questions of those involved to glean a clear understanding of the situation and ensure that assumptions are not made too broadly.
- Separate correlation from causation. An idea associated with a bad outcome does not necessarily mean the idea is bad.
- Learn from successes or failures, but don't assume that what happens in one instance always applies to the next or corollary situations.

Most often the "guilty" person is unaware of their guilt. To help prevent this from happening to you, maintain a relationship with someone you work with and know well (a boss, mentor, peer) who can "check your 6" (military parlance for looking out behind you). This person can alert you to potential issues where you are at risk of being unfairly branded.

Be one of the "cool kids," when someone or thing is being branded negatively due to an unwarranted association. Separate fact from fiction.

Hasty Generalization

Location: Focus group viewing room in Dallas, Texas.

Issue: Joe, the marketing manager of a lawn care products manufacturer, is viewing a focus group of lawn care service company owners. They are exploring landscapers' attitudes toward the design of power string trimmers—also known as "weed whackers"—a tool used to trim grass from driveways, walkways, fences, and other areas one does not want grass to cover.

> Terry (focus group moderator): *"Here are three examples of power trimmers."* [Terry places three power string trimmers on the conference table.] *"Let's first just talk about the physical design of these trimmers—what they look like, the shape of the trimmers—what are your thoughts about them?*

> Jack (focus group respondent): *"I like that switch on the side of the handle that controls the speed of the trimmer—that switch with the rabbit and turtle icons. It's easy to push with your thumb when you're trimming grass. It makes it easy to save gas when you don't need a lot of power, say, when you're trimming a sidewalk."*

> [Other focus group participants generally agree with Jack.]

> Joe (marketing manager): *"That makes a lot of sense. When we get back to the office, I'll make sure we relay that information to the design engineers. We need to keep the speed control switch where it is on our new generation of trimmers."*

Joe is using the findings from one focus group to make a decision about the design of his company's next generation power string trimmers. This sample size of just one focus group may not reflect the attitudes of most landscape service owners across the country.

Definition: A *Hasty Generalization* is one in which a person uses small and not necessarily representative samples from a given population to make a general statement about that population. A hasty generalization is a faulty inductive inference:

- Premise 1: X percent of observed P's possess characteristic Q.
- Premise 2: These observed P's are a small and not necessarily a representative sample of the population P.
- Conclusion: Therefore, X percent of *all* P's possess characteristic Q.

Discussion

Of course, it may be that the inference from a small sample turns out to be valid; however, the misjudgment behind this fallacy is that it is not *deductively valid.*

Recall that a deductively valid argument is one in which, if the premises of an argument are true, then the conclusion is *guaranteed* to be true. For example: (1) Socrates is a man; (2) All men are mortal; therefore (3) Socrates is mortal. This is a deductively valid argument because if (1) and (2) are true, (3) is guaranteed to be true. Not so for hasty generalizations. In our example, premises #1 and #2, even though true, do not guarantee the plausibility or truth of the conclusion.

Marketing managers, consciously or not, will sometimes employ hasty generalizations to support their own biases. (Politicians are famous for doing so.) More often, hasty generalizations reflect sloppy or lazy thinking and, if you can get your audience to agree with your point using this logical fallacy, this certainly can save you a lot of time conducting research to develop a stronger argument. It is also used by those trying to collect the "facts" needed to support their own agenda.

Of course, we don't want to throw the baby out with the bath water! Advertising uses the Hasty Generalization to appeal to viewers' emotions all the time. If you want to be sexually appealing, use Channel cologne or Old Spice aftershave, for example.

Dealing with Hasty Generalization

This is an easy fallacy to address. In the focus group example, often all you need to do is wait until the next focus group to discover that other respondents articulate different beliefs and intentions from the first and give face valid reasons for their position.

Regardless, the key to addressing this fallacy in the work place is simply to point out that a larger, more representative sample may provide a different answer. Management will have to decide whether or not the costs associated with getting larger and more representative samples are worth it. Clearly, organizations cannot research every question; and, sometimes, small sample sizes do corroborate the background knowledge of management.

Nonetheless, arguments supported by hasty generalizations stand on weak stilts. Strengthen these supports by replacing them with more representative and valid statistics.

Hypnotic Bait and Switch

Location: Power tools manufacturing company headquarters corporate board room.

Issue: The marketing team is assembled to discuss a strategy to counter the commoditization of power tools sold to companies in the large construction and building industries market.

Elsa (VP marketing) speaking to Liam (director of marketing): *"Your team has been studying recent trends in the large construction industry, especially with regard to price pressures and the lack of product differentiation in our industry. What are your recommendations?"*

Liam: *"As you know, over the past 10 years, it has been difficult if not impossible to stop the commoditization in our industry.* [Team members nod their heads in agreement.] *All of our patents have expired; as a result, competitors have been dropping their prices, and we've had to match them.* [All nod in agreement.] *This is putting pressure on our profits, and we need to act quickly.* [Many softly say 'yes' in agreement.] *So our recommendation is to continue to drop prices and offer a loyalty program where the more a contractor buys from us, they better the price they get."*

Anton (president): *"Everything you've said, Liam, is true* [other team members nod their heads in agreement and softly say 'yes']—*the most significant patents that help us differentiate our brand have expired; the competitors have been reducing their prices; and, yes, we've had to match them. And it is also true that we need to act quickly. I'm leaning toward agreeing with you."*

Liam may truly believe that his recommendation is the best course of action. But he has cloaked the weakness of his argument in rhetoric— language and speech designed to persuade an audience, irrespective of the truth of one's claims—by using "Hypnotic Bait and Switch."

Definition: *Hypnotic Bait and Switch* comes from the old sales strategy of getting the prospect to say "yes … yes … yes …," and then asking for the sale, as if the agreement to purchase whatever the salesperson is selling is a logical consequence of saying "yes" to the statements preceding "the close."

Discussion

The term *hypnotic* refers to the repetitive "yes" responses, expressed either silently or verbally by the audience to an argument. The person making the argument attempts to get the audience in a supportive frame of mind to later accept the argument's conclusion uncritically. In Liam's case, he wants to motivate the VP and president to say "yes" to his recommendation to drop prices.

This vignette is partially based on a case study of the Hilti company, which appears in a popular marketing research text book by Byron Sharp,[14] "Hilti: From Goods to Service Provision." In fact, Hilti did not drop its prices.

"Hilti responded by offering large building contractors a service whereby the contractor did not need to purchase the power tools outright. Instead, Hilti would guarantee to supply the required set of well-maintained tools every day to a client's construction site. In this way, the building contractor would not have to buy, own and maintain the power tools, which was attractive to them."

Dealing with Hypnotic Bait and Switch

Persons employing this fallacy to support their conclusions may or may not be aware of what they are doing. Often they are simply charismatic leaders or team members who are convinced they are right. However, anyone who has sold for a living at some point in their career should automatically recognize the buildup to the final "big" agreement. The time context of the aforementioned vignette is also important; if the meeting is at the conclusion of a long arduous period of study, then summarizing the small agreements to get to a final agreement may be warranted (and necessary to prevent ongoing navel gazing).

In our example, the best way to guard against being "hypnotized," is to have the team evaluate the logical link between Liam's premises and his conclusion by asking, *"Do your premises allow for only one conclusion—or are other options open to us, other than dropping our prices via a loyalty program?"* Another strategy might be to say something like, *"That's a viable strategy, given the premises you've laid out. Building upon what you've said, what other options might be open to us?"*

Inflation of Conflict

Situation: Sales managers are meeting at an offsite channel to discuss challenges to, and plans for, channel selling.

Issue: How, and how hard, should we go after Internet sales?
This conversation can go one of two ways:

Conversation 1:

Junker (sales): *"I don't think we should be investing our time with these Internet channels. We are not set up for it, and the trial run we did closed like, what, $300 in sales—not $300K, but $300.00. This is a waste of our time, and we need to kill our Internet sales initiative."*

Roberto (product management): *"But we need to think about how customers might behave with our competitors. I can go online to all of our competitors right now and shop for spare parts. Once I near the transaction point, I will get handed over to one of their dealers seamlessly. It's the wave of the future; we have to shape it or it will shape us."*

Donald (channel manager*): "Well, I see we don't have much common ground so, in the interest of time, I say we table this and move on to the next agenda item."*

Conversation 2:

Junker (sales): *"I don't think we should be investing our time with these Internet channels. We are not set up for it, and the trial run we did closed like, what, $3 million in sales—but we had modeled $4 million in the business case. Sounds like an under forecast of 25% to me. Failures like that waste our time, and we need to kill our Internet sales initiative."*

Roberto (product management): *"Wait, wait. It was $3.2 million on a business case of $3.8 million. More important, I can go online to all of our competitors and shop. It's the wave of the future; we have to shape it or it will shape us."*

Donald (channel manager): *"Well, I see we don't agree on the results of the pilot or the business case we signed up to achieve, except that we did not meet forecast. So, in the interest of time, I say we table this and move on to the next agenda item."*

Definition: The premise of an *Inflation of Conflict* is: Person A and Person B disagree on Subject Y. Conclusion: Therefore we cannot have a meaningful dialog on Subject Y. In both conversations, lack of consensus on the subject of Internet sales led to an Inflation of Conflict by Donald. He makes the disagreement between Junker and Roberto a bigger deal than it should be as an excuse to delay decision making.

Discussion

These conflicts tend to happen often in marketing, because marketers are often expected to be the internal change agent. Data, universal understanding of the *market texture* (that's our word for what other industries might describe as texture, architecture, or landscape—the sum of marketing factors that make up the market environment), and a common analysis of the problems or root causes usually result in people holding positions based on what they have experienced or believe. When people hold a position for emotional reasons, it may not always be readily defensible, and conflict ensues. This conflict tends to be personal and less about facts, thus inflating the conflict to the point where it does not make sense for anyone to risk taking on the conversation. Someone with a lot of organizational or political power or a stubborn streak can become a serial inflator of conflict.

Dealing with Inflation of Conflict

Inflation of Conflict is easily resolved with a deflection to data or a simple suggestion to "let the data speak." With any luck, there is some data or factual information readily at hand that can deflate the conflict and avert a delay or deferral.

But what if data are not available? The obvious answer is to suggest collecting and analyzing some. However, proceed with caution, as the parties who inflated the conflict know or at least have a feeling that the data is not available or the analysis is not clear. In this case, it is critical to do a few things. First, get those in the conflict to agree on the minimum set of data required to make the decision. Second, gather the data quickly. Finally, agree to return to the subject as soon as the data is available. The latter point is critical because, with no agreement to return to the table ASAP, then the parties who have used the Inflation of Conflict fallacy to their advantage in the short term will make it stick.

Logical Inconsistency

Situation: Teleconference between IT, sales, and marketing to review system priorities.

Issue: On which projects should we focus our scarce IT resources?

> Jameson (sales leader): *"We really need to put our efforts into a sales force automation (SFA) tool to track our leads and put some rigor into the management of the sales force. I think it is something we can get up and running out of the box with a SaaS solution and, therefore, would require few man-hours and primarily just an expense budget."*

> Guinness (marketing leader): *"I know you have been asking for that for a long time, but we really need IT to upgrade the website infrastructure*

and include the dealer locator programs Bailey has been having his team write. Our website is looking dated, and almost everyone else has a dealer locator on their site."

Bailey (IT leader): *"I have not seen a business case for the SFA tool you are asking for, Jameson, so until I see one, I think we should continue with the in-house work on our web properties and integrate that dealer locator Guinness has been asking for. We've spent a lot on these projects and it will take a lot more to get these done, so they need to be our focus."*

Jameson: *"So, you require a business case from me but not Guinness? When did he give you his business case? I don't remember seeing it. Please share."*

In the preceding scenario, Bailey is being logically inconsistent because he is asking Jameson for a business case to move forward, but admits that there has already been investment and will continue to be more in the future.

Definition: Typically, *Logical Inconsistency* has statements in the argument that, as asserted, cannot possibly both be true:

- Side A of a card: "The other side of this card is true."
- Side B of a card: "The other side of this card is false."

Discussion

Not all inconsistencies are as classic as Yogi Berra's, "A nickel ain't worth a dime anymore." When dealing with people in business situations, identifying how inconsistencies come about is not as clear-cut. Sometimes it's policies that are inconsistent or applications of practices, and so on.

In the aforementioned scenario, the IT leader is inconsistently applying the practice of asking for a business case. He requires it in Jamison's case, but ignores it for Guinness. (Naturally, we would never accuse IT of working on in-house pet projects that have no business case over using "their" money to purchase an off-the-shelf solution that is nearly not as much fun to play with, even though its business case is virtually axiomatic.)

Requirements such as "we need a business case" always sound logical (and might make the speaker appear to have learned a thing or two in grad school) but, when applied inconsistently, are more likely roadblocks to win what is often an emotional or opinion-based argument. Or it is used in situations where there is apathy against rigor or a desire not to change.

Dealing with Logical Inconsistency

In the aforementioned example, Jameson has started down the right path. Knowing that logical inconsistency is driven either by emotion or by lack of intelligence/enlightenment, it is best to determine which. In the case of emotions, it is important, as always, to take care with the human element (and the political) to make sure that any further argument is productive rather than destructive. If it is merely lack of intellect or data as the root cause, then the simplest solution is the one we suggest for many logical fallacies in this book: probe, ask questions, force analysis, and so on.

Lying with Statistics

Location: Sales manager's office of a national power equipment manufacturer.

Issue: The sales manager and VP of marketing are reviewing a statistical report on a new territory where they are considering expanding the distribution of their company's lawn mower line.

Joann (VP of marketing): *"What is your assessment of the potential in this geographic area?"*

Mike (sales manager): *"As you know, one of the most predictive factors affecting our sales is the household income in the territory. We like to see that number above $45,000. And the average for this territory is $46,400, which gives us a good margin above our requirement."*

Joann: *"That sounds good. Let's go ahead with the plan and talk to some distributors that serve that geography."*

(Two years later)

Joann: *"Mike, sales are not what we expected in this new territory. What's wrong?"*

Mike: *"I'm not sure. Household income levels are where we wanted them to be. Did we do enough advertising?"*

Both Joann and Mike were fooled by the *average* household income level of $46,400. Had they examined the data on the distribution of household income more carefully, they would have discovered that the *median* household income—the income level at which 50 percent of households are above and 50 percent are below—was only $30,000, which misses by a wide mark their belief that the "average" household income should be near $45,000.

Definition: This is an example of *Lying with Statistics*, a fallacy in which statistics are misused—intentionally or not—to support an argument.

Discussion

Perhaps the most famous book ever written on this subject was, *How to Lie with Statistics*, written by Darrell Huff in 1954, which you can still purchase on Amazon.com. And, although our book is not intended to be a comprehensive discussion of this topic, no book on logical fallacies would be complete without some space allocated to how easily one can incorrectly use statistics to support a position—to lie with statistics.

The most pervasive example of how statistics can mislead is with respect to averages, or measures of central tendency in a set of data. When you use the term *average* in daily life, it seems like something "we all understand" (which fallacy is that?). In reality, there are three different ways to look at averages; three different statistical measures of central tendency:

- *Mean* is simply the addition of all numbers with respect to a given factor (e.g., household incomes in a geographic area), divided by the number of observations. In the previous example, the mean household income is $46,400.
- *Median* is the number for which half the observations are larger and half smaller which, in the preceding example, is $30,000.

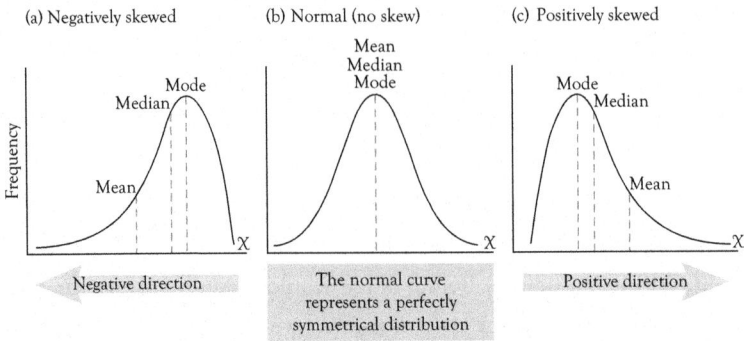

Figure 5.2 Mean, median, and mode

- *Mode* is the number that appears with the greatest frequency—$25,000 in the aforementioned example.

You can easily use Excel or a statistical software package to calculate these basic statistics.

Most often, news releases and marketing research reports give the *mean* statistic, often because it is the simplest to explain. But, as you can see, the mean or "average" statistic can be misleading if the distribution of the data is skewed, as shown in Figure 5.2.

In our vignette, Figure 5.2 denotes the problem. This distribution of household incomes is skewed in a positive direction because a handful of households have relatively large incomes, which causes the mean to be larger than the median.

Dealing with Lying with Statistics

Clearly, with any "average" statistic, you should ask to see both the mean and median and, if they differ significantly, perhaps even ask to see the raw distribution of the data plotted, as in Figure 5.2.

Using statistics to support marketing decisions is generally sound management. "Having the data" implies a greater degree of rigor was applied to solving the question at hand. However, as we have seen in this very simple case, misinterpretation of the data due to misuse of statistics can provide an end result that is worse (or no better) than simply following your gut instinct. And sometimes statistics can mislead—intentionally or unintentionally.

The old adage is unfortunately true: *"There are liars, damn liars, and statisticians."* To protect yourself—as well as insure you don't inadvertently "lie" using a statistics—purchase a copy of Huff's classic book. Better yet, purchase a used college statistics book and become familiar with both the strengths and weakness of statistics.

Finally, when confronted with statistics to support a decision, use them to inform, not to make the decision. Take the time to get familiar with the data, ask questions of it—at least until that magic day when the "decision making machine" is so finely tuned that you can just turn the crank.

Misleading Vividness

Location: The headquarters of Apex Brands, a large spirits distributorship.

Issue: The regional sales manager and the company's VP of marketing are discussing the recent loss of a large retail account.

> Sherrill (regional sales manager): *[Speaking in an emotional, anxious tone]; "Alex, the buyer at Choice Brands Liquor Stores was all in a huff this afternoon. He tells me that they've seen a steady increase in their ready-to-drink sales, and that he needs to switch distributors to one of our competitors that has a broader line in that category."*

> Jean (VP of marketing): *"So we lost the account?"*

> Sherrill: *"Yes, and boy was he dramatic. He took me to several of their stores and showed me the end-cap displays and shelf displays of the new ready-to-drink brands and flavors that his new distributor is supplying. He insisted that I take pictures of them and send them to you ... check your email and you can see them. Some even have special lighting surrounding the displays that make the colors on the bottles and the liquid inside them bounce off the packaging. It is impressive."*

This is both a dramatic and, with the cell phone pictures, vivid description of losing an account. But does it offer a good reason for Apex Brands to widen its line of ready-to-drink brands?

Definition: *Misleading Vividness* plays on a melodramatic and striking event to justify an argument in the absence of any reliable data to the contrary.

Discussion

Misleading Vividness plays on one's emotions and subjective assessments of risk to support an argument. Jean knows something is terribly wrong, just by the emotional tone of Sherrill's voice. But, as we discussed in the Appeal to Emotion fallacy, the best arguments are those that are clothed in reason and evidence—not emotion.

Inherent in this Misleading Vividness is an implied premise that comes from the social science discipline known as "behavioral economics"—that people often overestimate the probability of dramatic and vivid events occurring versus more common, everyday events. For example, death by tornado or earthquake is viewed more likely than dying from a fall. We are six times more likely to die from a fall than in a plane, yet people are more afraid to fly than walk.[15] This is called the *availability heuristic* in behavioral economics:

> The tendency to overestimate the likelihood of events with greater 'availability' in memory, which can be influenced by how recent the memories are or how unusual or emotionally charged they may be.[16]

Sherrill's argument plays on this behavioral economics concept: Although not stated directly, she implies that there is high probability that Apex will lose other accounts because she relates her story in an emotional and vivid manner, rather than if she had simply sent Jean a non-emotional e-mail, *without the pictures*, relaying the facts of the situation.

Emotion in business is a good thing. And almost anyone who has sold for a living can relate to the raw emotions felt when an account is lost. Likewise, who hasn't said that "a picture is worth 1,000 words?" Supporting claims with visual evidence helps to quickly and often more correctly explain things. The problem in the previous vignette isn't that emotion and visual evidence were used, but that that they inadvertently take the place of all the other factors that may have resulted in the loss of the account.

Dealing with Misleading Vividness

When confronted with Misleading Vividness, the best advice is to take a time-out. People who use this fallacy typically are unaware of what they are doing—they are acting in the moment. Acknowledge that person's emotions, but, also encourage her to ask the following questions:

- How does the proposed argument square with what is already known?
- What evidence, outside of the emotional plea, supports the argument's conclusion?
- How common is the event in question?

Remember: Keep cool. Emotion is not an argument.

Nirvana

Location: Workshop on an aftermarket pricing strategy for next year.

Issue: How can we achieve maximum returns by optimizing pricing? The pricing leader is showing a mathematical relationship on a grease board that relates profits (a) to the percentage of customers paying the highest price for a product (b).

Mackenzie (pricing leader): *"Our greatest profit comes from this point on the curve where each buyer is paying the most they are willing to before switching to competitors or alternate solutions, not a penny less."*

Clifton (channel sales leader): *"I understand your theory on price maximization but I'm not certain it is practical in this application. We can't manage a different price list for every dealer. We need to keep it simple by charging one price."*

Mackenzie: *"Look, our mandate is to get the maximum returns for our owners, the shareholders, and management has chartered the work on pricing to do exactly what I am suggesting, maximizing our profit from each transaction through pricing effectiveness. If we don't go after a business process and set of tools that achieves this flexibility, we might as well not be here."*

Mackenzie is advocating a state of nirvana for pricing strategy professionals. On the other side, Clifton is an advocate of compromise through simplicity for the tacticians.

Definition: The *Nirvana* fallacy goes something like this: X is a current state (or a proposed state) and Y is the theoretical optimum state. Therefore X should be discarded as an option because it's not Y.

Discussion

Whether it is in price, promotion, place, or product, there will always be theories and theoreticians in marketing that define for us the pinnacle of perfection, or how something should work. These nirvana states are neither wrong nor bad. They are just usually not practical.

The nirvana state should be a reference in our preparation of strategy, but not a filter for our tactical selection. Strategy and strategic thinking are preparations for the marketing battle, but as German military strategist Helmuth von Moltke said, *"No battle plan survives contact with the enemy."*[17] Likewise, the theoretical nirvana of our marketing strategy will not survive implementation, and we need to be ready for that.

Dealing with Nirvana

You may have heard these two sayings: *"Don't let perfection be the enemy of good,"* and *"Don't delay for perfection when we have good enough now."* These are the moderating voices that need to be used when encountering the Nirvana fallacy. Acknowledge that you do not disagree with the pursuit of perfection, but that you just want to be the moderate voice of reason advocating progress, even if nirvana can't be achieved.

A practice becoming popular in the IT space is called "Agile." This practice may be instructive and informative for those of us in the marketing space as well, especially as there is so much more crossover between information technology and marketing than ever before. Actually IT may not survive as a stand-alone discipline because it will be the foundation of all the other business disciplines. For example, how silly would it be for a business to have a "Math Department"? Math resources and expertise need to be available in all departments, not necessarily "shared" across departments.

Agile is really a philosophy that says we should iterate our way quickly to nirvana instead of finding the silver bullet to get us there now. This seems eminently practical in a world that is speeding up and increasing in volatility. From AgileMethodology.org:[18]

> *"Agile methodology is an alternative to traditional project management, typically used in software development. It helps teams respond to unpredictability through incremental, iterative work cadences, known as sprints. Agile methodologies are an alternative to waterfall, or traditional sequential development."*

But don't settle for good if better or best is within practical reach. There are times when the pendulum can swing too far away from—or the compass of other leaders cannot point high enough to—perfection. In those cases, you may be called upon to be a change agent and follow the advice of another famous German military strategist (how come they are all German?), Carl von Clausewitz, *"If the leader is filled with high ambition and if he pursues his aims with audacity and strength of will, he will reach them in spite of all obstacles."*[19]

No True Scotsman

Location: Marketing video conference call.

Issue: Review of recent consumer insights study on the Supergreen lawn care fertilizer. Do we like the results?

> Jordie (segment general manager): *"So if I remember right, we decided that, before going ahead with your promotional plan for Supergreen, we would have your outside firm research the possible consumer behaviors to see if the plan could potentially result in the market share gain we have targeted."*

> Krista (marketing leader): *"Well, I had Terrence run the study like we have done several times before, but his conclusion is dissatisfying. His*

results show about half the gain we have targeted. But I think we should follow our gut and go ahead anyway because Terrence really isn't an expert in this consumer segment and so I am suspicious of his results."

Jordie: *"When you say 'our gut' you really mean 'your gut' don't you? The reason we agreed to a research study by 'your guy' originally was to break the tie between my gut and your gut. Didn't we just do this?"*

Krista put faith in "her guy," but does not like the results, so she is disavowing him as not a true "Scotsman."

Definition: The *No True Scotsman* fallacy goes like this: All X are Y. We found an X which is not Y. Therefore, it must not really be an X.

Discussion

The name of this fallacy is rather fun, a little less dry than some of the others. Think of it this way: We know that all Scotsman are frugal, right? But what about Gordon Ramsay, the famous TV Chef from Scotland who owns a Malibu mansion? He must not be a true Scotsman.

In the preceding scenario, Krista hired "her guy" to provide research that would help her make an informed decision. Obviously, he was good enough for her to hire: X (any good research study) will provide Y (a corroboration of my beliefs). But then, when the information came back contrary to the foregone conclusion of all X are Y—any good research will support my beliefs—her position shifts to it must not really be an X (it must not be the right research).

Krista: "Terrence is a Scotsman because he does good research."

Jordie: "Terrence's research was not good—it did not support my beliefs."

Krista: "Therefore, he is no true Scotsman."

Dealing with No True Scotsman

There are really two possible failures here. First, not all X are really Y. Second, we do not want to accept the consequences of the logic. Both failure modes need to be explored.

Failure 1: Things are not always what they seem. Rarely are *all* X really Y. Krista should have done her due diligence to ensure that Terrence was the right researcher to conduct the proposed study. She should have gotten a few additional bids to better assess the best firm for this particular study.

Failure 2: We need to live up to the consequences of the contracts we make. Krista agreed to a "tie-breaker" and she lost. Now she needs to live up to it, accept the findings, and move on.

That none of this book's authors is a true Scotsman does not mean you should not take our advice.

Non Sequitur

Location: Product pipeline planning meeting for an auto parts manufacturer.

Issue: Where should we launch—as part of our Original equipment manufacturer (OEM) engine or in the aftermarket?

Abe (strategic customer market leader): *"We were just out at SEMA* (Specialty Equipment Marketing Association, the predominant aftermarket products trade show) *and the fuel economy 'chip' is exactly the kind of product people eat up out there in their new products demo area. I think we should launch this on our next transmission for OEM installation in Freightpuller's new truck going into production next year."*

Angela (VP aftermarket): *"Abe, that's a non sequitur. You just said yourself that people would eat this up in the aftermarket and then you suggest we give it to Freightpuller as part of an original package? What you said does not make any sense—unless you are planning to charge Freightpuller aftermarket margins, which I doubt."*

Abe: *"But our quality and delivery has been so poor recently, I'm looking to give them extra value to keep them on our side. You can release it in the aftermarket later."*

Angela: *"Sorry Abe, but again you are not making sense. Freightpuller won't know the value of it when you give it to them. I have a better Idea. You let me release it at $1,000 and 80% margin. The market eats it up* *and then you give it to Freightpuller for $200 and they will be really happy with the $800 you just gave them."*

Definition: The word "non sequitur" is Latin for "it does not follow." When someone is making a *Non Sequitur* fallacy, they conclude X, but then give data supporting Y or, in reverse, give data supporting Y and then conclude X. Note that although all formal fallacies may be characterized as non sequiturs, the term can also apply to informal fallacies—such as the one in this vignette—in which the content of the argument is simply illogical.

Discussion

In the aforementioned scene you might have thought that the argument was going well. The product should be popular. But the conclusion that the company should release a product in an OEM channel using analysis suggesting that the product will be popular in the aftermarket does not follow.

Non sequitur fallacies can be deceiving to those who are not experts in the topic. In the previous scene, it took someone who knew the differences between first-fit and aftermarket channels to recognize the logical disconnect. Otherwise, the logic seemed sound: "The product will be well received, so let's release it."

In marketing decision making we are not always looking for "the" answer (as we are in 2 + 2), but for the "best" answer, which means, by definition, that there will be multiple acceptable answers. But there will only be one "best decision." The best answer is the one where the logic follows "best." Second or third best are non sequiturs in a business context.

Dealing with Non Sequitur

Stay awake. Become an expert in the subject matter. Question arguments: *"Really? 2 + 2 = 5*—are you sure?" Keep looking for the best conclusion. Everyone should want the best conclusion for the business. It's in everyone's best interest (at least in the long run), so it's usually not offensive to probe for the best answer, test alternatives, and ask a lot of questions.

Poisoning the Well

Location: Lobby of a hotel where the leadership team is having an off-site annual planning session.

Issue: What product developments should be in our plan for the tactical (one-year) and strategic (five-year) horizons?

James (product development leader): *"Toby is going to propose we extend ourselves into software again. We failed five years ago when we tried that, and five years before, and five years before that."*

Edwina (president): *"Toby is new. Maybe he has a new approach."*

James: *"He's going to try to snow you with some of the MBA BS on market forces and his customer insights and a balance of risk and reward etc. He hasn't been through six market cycles like I have. Trust me, don't let him convince you with his pretty plots."*

James is in the process of "poisoning the well" with Edwina. What's worse is that Toby isn't even there to defend himself.

Definition: *Poisoning the Well* is a logical fallacy committed before any evidence can even be presented. It is essentially introducing/forcing a false bias even before the argument begins.

The fallacy can be stated as: X is going to make a decision about Y. But before X can hear the facts about Y, she is biased to think/behave illogically.

Discussion

In this situation, James is poisoning the well for Toby. Here, the well is Edwina's opinion. If James were doing the same thing with others on the leadership team they would also be considered "the well." He is attempting to tilt the scales against the presentation Toby is about to make before the logic can even be presented. Toby may have a great discussion prepared, but if James is successful in getting others not to listen, then his view will prevail. For this tactic to work, Edwina needs to let herself be poisoned. If she listens, then she too is committing a Poisoning the Well fallacy.

Poisoning the well is not limited to boardroom decision makers. In marketing, the same failure mode can show up in the research phase. If a research treatment (e.g., a product concept to be tested), respondent selection criteria, or survey question wording biases the sample or the data then, in effect, the "well" has been poisoned. Sometimes it's actually done on purpose in the field of behavior economics to learn more about the subject or psychology. For example, behavioral economists have demonstrated that subtly reminding female research subjects that they are girls right before a math test results in lower scores. No one understands exactly how this works, but it's a perfect example of poisoning the well.

Dealing with Poisoning the Well

This fallacy can be very nefarious, as illustrated by James and Edwina. It is akin to political backstabbing. James is so underhanded that he attacks Toby's argument even before it can begin and without him even being there to defend himself.

Unfortunately, the only sure way to win is to be an expert in workplace politics. However, even if you are not, add some good fundamentals of marketing rhetoric (sound data, logical analysis, persuasive presentation) to your defense when launching a poisoned well parry. And one more thing: Know who the "well" is and aim your rhetoric there.

Now, as we explained, you can also make a fallacious error in poisoning the well when you perform research. The way to deal with this is to make sure your methods are sound and, if you are not a research expert, get one involved. Don't perform surgery if you are not a surgeon.

Prejudicial Language

Location: Sales conference room.

Issue: The sales and marketing team are discussing next year's advertising strategy.

Andi (sales manager): *"Any reasonable person would agree that we need to increase our social media presence. That's what all our competitors are doing, and I have yet to see a customer without a smart phone."*

Grantham (marketing manager): *"That's what your advertising agency claims. I believe that any right-thinking person has to acknowledge the effect that our sales force has had talking belly-to-belly with our customers and prospects. I say we keep the budget just the way we had it last year."*

Although we cannot be sure about whether Andi or Grantham are drawing truthful conclusions, they are definitely using loaded and emotive language to support their arguments. And that, as much as anything, is a reason not to believe what they are saying.

Definition: The *Prejudicial Language* fallacy occurs when one party uses loaded and emotive terms to strengthen an argument, as opposed to using facts and truth-conducive reasoning.

Discussion

Prejudicial language is often used—sometimes unconsciously—to intimidate one's audience into agreement. It frames arguments by linking them to certain values, preconceptions, or moral considerations. Consider these examples of phrases or terms that signal this fallacy in action:

"All good marketers …"	"Companies that want to succeed …"	"Any reasonable person …"
"They claim …"	"A smart person …"	"Any real marketer …"
"People in the know …"	"If you think through this carefully you have to agree …"	"We don't want to sleepwalk our way [into doing or committing to something] …"
"The empty suits say …"	"They [another department in an organization] are like a bull in a china shop when they say …"	"If they believe that, I've got a bridge to sell them."

In our vignette, the terms *any reasonable person* and *any right-thinking person* are examples of prejudicial language. This type of language isn't hard to identify and it probably makes the hair on the back of your neck stand up because it is often demeaning and counterproductive.

Dealing with Prejudicial Language

Sometimes using prejudicial language is appropriate. For example, if a team has agreed on a course of action that is well supported by facts and evidence, there is nothing wrong with using this fallacy for motivational purposes—*"Only a world class team could have done the kind of research and strategic planning that we've done for the upcoming fiscal year."*

Otherwise, as enthusiastic as we can be about our suggestions and recommendations, dialing down the emotion and dialing up objectivity and evidence is the best way to form marketing arguments. After all, that's what smart people do!

Proof by Intimidation

Location: Marketing conference room of Superior Pet Foods.

Issue: Apex (contract marketing research firm) is reviewing the results of a study that investigated price-feature trade-offs for a pet food company's redesigned puppy food. Jerry (Superior's marketing research manager) introduces Linda, Apex's senior analyst, who has a PhD in experimental psychology from Harvard.

Linda: *"We employed an advanced research method called conjoint anal-ysis for this study. By having respondents tell us their preferences for an orthogonally designed set of prototype dry pet food products, we can infer how much they are willing to pay for certain characteristics of this new product that you think may give your company a competitive edge in this market. For example, we can examine consumers' preferences for this new product at various prices if it contains certain cuts of meat—chicken vs. lamb—or certain vegetables, such as corn vs. carrots."*

Jerry: *"Apex has developed a proprietary market share simulator that pro-vides insight into how the new product's market share may change and its corresponding profitability to us. Their algorithm is quite impressive."*

Michele (Superior's chief marketing officer): *"That sounds pretty amaz-ing and highly scientific. I'm anxious to learn more."*

Notice some of the words that Linda and Jerry are using: *PhD, experimental psychology, Harvard, conjoint analysis, orthogonally, proprietary, simulator,* and *algorithm.* Intentionally or not, these words have the power to intimidate an audience. Who wants to question, let alone argue with, a PhD from Harvard?

Definition: In *Proof by Intimidation,* the presenter or what is being presented is potentially intimidating to an audience, thus promoting underscrutinized or uncritical acceptance of an argument.

Discussion

The terms that Jerry and Linda are using are not jargon (made up words or phrases designed to impress). Rather, they're using legitimate terms from real fields of study. If you have a background in experimental psychology or advanced marketing research methods, these terms are familiar to you, but they probably sound like "Greek" to others. These terms might impress, but they also can intimidate.

Proof by Intimidation often occurs in technical fields. Those with technical backgrounds use technical jargon to keep nontechnical coworkers off their backs.

Dealing with Proof by Intimidation

On an emotional level, try to guard against being intimidated when terminology is unfamiliar, as the language may have been used innocently with no intent to intimidate. But such terminology can still be critically examined. Here are some suggestions:

- Separate jargon from legitimate English. For example, the following phrases are examples of jargon: *paradigm shift, leverage a best practice, join a tiger team, core competency, buy-in, SWAT Team, empower, and drinking the Kool-Aid.*[20] These terms should not intimidate you, and Michele in the previous scenario has every reason to question the competency of the person using them, even if she does have a PhD from Harvard. Sometimes people use jargon as shorthand for concepts that are complex and require more words to describe. But often they are used by people who don't know what they are talking about, who want to impress you, or who are attempting to intimidate you.

- Ask for clarification. In the aforementioned scenario, Michele should have had Linda explain what "orthogonal" means and why it is meaningful to the subject at hand. In this case, "orthogonal" is a property of a research design that makes the findings more valid. And validity is essential to good research.

- Probe for whether there are any negative associations with a particular term you find intimidating, and how that association may affect the credibility of the user's argument. For example, "proprietary" means the method that Apex is using probably has not been peer-reviewed, so only they know how it works (or doesn't). You have to take their word that the method is valid. In this situation, Michele would need to question the facts and premises upon which Apex feels that their proprietary method is indeed valid.

Red Herring

Location: Veterinarian medical manufacturer's marketing off-site strategy meeting.

Issue: Prioritizing marketing mix expenditures.

David (VP marketing): *"On the topic of our sales effort, our research indicates that our sales reps are simply not as effective at closing the sale as our competitors' sales reps are. I'm suggesting, therefore, that we hire Sales Excellence World Wide to come in and help our sales reps improve and refine their selling skills."*

Terry (director of marketing): *"The more serious problems facing our company are developing and launching our web strategy. You think we're behind our competitors on closing the sale; we don't even have a chance if our prospects don't know who we are. This is where we should be focusing our resources."*

David is talking about sales call effectiveness and offering a recommendation on how it can be improved. Terry is trying to change the topic and says nothing about the validity of David's argument.

Definition: A *Red Herring* diverts the audience's attention away from the argument at hand and onto a different topic, implying that the original argument is not worth the time to discuss.

Discussion

This fallacy incorporates the metaphor of a red herring—originally used in England to train dogs for fox hunting—as an indicator of bad logic. Trainers wanted their dogs to follow the fox's scent and not be distracted during the hunt, so they dragged particularly pungent dead fish—often an overly cured herring—across the fox's path as part of the dogs' training regimen. In the previous scenario, Terry diverts the discussion away from sales training to the company's web strategy.

The Red Herring should not be confused with the "Straw Man" fallacy. Whereas the former seeks to change the topic of conversation, the latter attempts to misrepresent another's argument in a way that sets it up for ridicule. Had Terry used the Straw Man fallacy, he might have said: *"Heck, if they take Friday afternoons off, fewer sales calls will result in fewer sales, regardless of how good they are."* Here, Terry is misrepresenting David's argument as a means to discredit it. He's saying that the cause of low sales is the laziness of the company's lazy sales reps, not their professional selling skills.

As explained by Kevin deLaplante in his online course on critical thinking:[21]

So, putting all this together, you commit the red herring fallacy when, in an argument, you divert attention away from the main issue or the main line of argumentation by introducing something that *changes the subject*, that *raises a new issue* that isn't relevant to the preceding line of discussion.

The fallacy really occurs when you then conclude something from this different issue, or presume that some conclusion has been established, and use this to claim that you've won the argument or said something relevant about the original argument.

Dealing with Red Herring

The obvious advice here is, *"Don't take the bait!"* When confronted with this fallacy, the arguer is tempted to quickly address the red herring and then return to her original argument. The problem with this approach is that it often doesn't work. It's like getting caught in quicksand. You address one red herring, and your challenger throws down another. And another.

A best tactic is to call a time out. Clarify the real topic of discussion. In the aforementioned scenario, there are two issues on the table: (1) how to improve the selling effectiveness of the sales reps and (2) the relative impact on sales of improving sales rep performance versus developing an effective web strategy. Those in the meeting need to agree on which topic to discuss and not combine the two.

Don't let red herrings distract your attention. Keep your eye on the fox.

Regression to the Mean

Location: The Acme Boat manufacturer's conference room.

Issue: Acme Boat's management is discussing how to increase the company's share of its retail distributors' business.

David (vice president marketing): *"Perhaps we should interview our best and worst retail distributors—the top 5% and bottom 5% in terms of the percentage of their retail boat sales that are our brand. Terry, perhaps you can put together a list of those distributors based on last year's data."*

Terry (marketing research manager): *"That's pretty easy to do. I can get that list from IT."*

David: *"Then go out an interview those distributors and see what the top end is doing differently or better than the bottom 5%. We will use those findings to set our distributor strategy for the upcoming season."*

David's idea is a good one—compare and contrast the best and worst performers in their retail distribution channel; however, defining the "best" and "worst" distributors based on one season's data exposes Acme to the "Regression to the Mean" fallacy—the best performers this year may not be the best performers over the long run. Structuring the sample this way will likely lead to biased results.

Definition: *Regression to the Mean* is reflected in a condition in which an object—for example, a boat dealership—is measured on a given statistic—for example, the percentage of Acme boats sold by a dealership in a calendar year—where the value of that statistic takes on an extreme value relative to the normal range of values it will take on over a relevant period of time.

Discussion

Regression to the Mean is sometimes referred to as the *Sports Illustrated* fallacy. An athlete has a great season and finds herself the subject of *Sports Illustrated's* front cover, only to experience diminished performance the next season and become the butt of sports pundits' jokes. The athlete's performance over time regresses to the person's average performance. This fallacy was first pointed out in business by Horace Secrist over 80 years ago:

> In the midst of the Great Depression, Northwestern University statistics professor Horace Secrist made a great discovery. It was one that had the potential to provide insight into the nation's economic woes and perhaps even put America back on the road to prosperity. Secrist traced the fortunes of 49 department stores between 1920 and 1930, measuring their ratio of net profit or loss to net sales. He divided these stores into four groups—from lowest 1920 profits to highest 1920 profits. Secrist took the average performance of each of the four groups and traced it over the decade. Stores with higher than average profits performed steadily worse throughout the decade, whereas stores with lower than average performance performed steadily better. The overall trend was

clear to Secrist: The performances of the businesses were converging on mediocrity.[22]

In hindsight, this fallacy of reasoning seems obvious; yet it has tripped up some popular business pundits such as *Good to Great*'s author Jim Collins:

In a 2008 issue of The *Academy of Management Perspectives,* scholars observed that Collins' "great" companies failed to outperform the S&P 500 in the decade following publication of his book. Although the commentators pointed out several flaws in Collins' methodology, none pointed out the fact that focusing on a small subset of high-performing companies is a recipe for observing declining performance in subsequent years. This was analogous to Secrist focusing on only the top quartile of department stores.[23]

Why do we sometimes unconsciously gravitate to using Regression to the Mean? Perhaps it just seems logical to assume that what happened in the past will happen in the future. Or maybe we are just too lazy to analyze top versus bottom performers over time.

Dealing with Regression to the Mean

This is an easy fallacy to correct if you are the one making it. Anytime you set forth to label or investigate the "best" or the "worst" of anything—distributors, sales representatives, products, services—examine their performance over several time periods before concluding what is "good" and "bad."

If a coworker makes the Regression to the Mean fallacy—probably unknowingly—suggest they look at the performance metric over time. In the previous vignette, Terry might have said, *"That's a good idea, David, and it might also be a good idea to see if the top 5% of our distributors last year were also in the top 5% the year before that. Some distributors could have just have had unrepeatable good or bad luck."*

Comparing the best versus the worst performers in any aspect of business activity can provide useful insights in developing marketing strategy.

But when doing this, remember the following baseball analogy: Baseball players with batting averages of 0.300 or higher in any season are 80 percent more likely to have lower batting averages in subsequent seasons.[24]

Relative Privation

Location: Corporate boardroom.

Issue: The president is completing his presentation of the company's first marketing plan to the board of directors.

> Rolf (president): [Concluding his presentation]: *"That summarizes the presentation of our first marketing plan. Just think, up until today, our company never had a formal marketing plan. This plan gives us direction that we've never had before and we can be more efficient in all of our efforts."*

[Board members nod their heads in agreement.]

> Agatha (board member): *"Compared to not having a marketing plan, I agree that we're much better off. Now we have a strategy to grow market share, which we haven't had before."*

It *may* be true that the company is better off with its first marketing plan, but the reasons for making this claim should not be made on the basis of "relative privation" logic. The plan's quality needs to be examined on its own merits.

Definition: *Relative Privation* is sometimes called the "It could be worse, it could be better" fallacy. If you want a given scenario to be perceived as better than it is, compare it to something worse. Conversely, if you want something to be perceived worse than it is, compare it to something better. "Eat your carrots. Think of all the starving children in Africa," is an example of the Relative Privation fallacy many of us heard as kids.

Discussion

Resorting to relative privation is often an excuse for lazy thinking. To make an argument more appealing, you can refer to a worst-case scenario. *"My plan is better because, if we didn't have a plan, we'd be worse off."*

Conversely, you can critique another's argument by comparing it to the perfect scenario: *"That's a good direct marketing idea, but you're only projecting a 5% response rate. Why can't we get a 15% response rate?"*

Dealing with Relative Privation

Any comparison of one scenario or argument to another scenario or argument must be appropriate to the situation. In the preceding vignette, the fact that the company never had a formal marketing plan is not a good argument supporting the value of the current plan, which needs to be assessed on its own merits.

If a colleague critiques one of your ideas using the Relative Privation fallacy, ask:

- *"How can we learn from the example you gave, to make my idea better?"*
- *"How does your example relate to my idea?"*
- *"How are the conditions surrounding your example similar to the conditions we're dealing with in my example?"*

Doing this is better than doing nothing!

Scapegoating

Location: Corporate conference room.

Issue: How to approach the market realities of new environmental legislation.

"Near-Term" Timmy (business unit leader): *"These new environmental regulations deliver no value to the consumer and are just another example of the government meddling in our industry and raising costs on the consumer. I have no idea how we are going to convince consumers to purchase our products after this transition. We should fight this."*

PR Paul (communications leader): *"We did have that huge spill two decades ago and our reputation is still recovering from it. But I agree this could be our opening, no one likes the government. This should be easy to hang on them. As you said, this is more of their meddling, let's make sure they look like the bad guy here. That way we look like we go down fighting at our customers' side and are 'real sorry we have to raise your prices but the evil government made us ....'"*

Consultant Cathy (strategy leader): *"Is there reason to believe we are at a disadvantage versus the competition with a new technical solution? Do we think they will solve the dilemma of this new regulatory regime better than us? If we don't respond technically as well as the competition—they have the same playing field as us—then we only have to blame ourselves. You are trying to blame the regulators when the facts remain that we compete against our competition and not the regulators. We should view this as a new opportunity to beat the completion. Let's get on the forward foot and build and sell a better mouse trap rather than complain about our cheese getting eaten."*

Timmy wants an easy way out. As Paul states they contributed to the regulatory environment they face, but really it's easier to blame the government than it is to actually improve.

Definition: *Scapegoating* is a means to deflect an argument. It is smoke and mirrors (and who knows more about smoke and mirrors than Marketing?) It is typically used in a case where by combining the power of suggestion and the bandwagon effect (suggesting a common enemy is the source of the problem) an alternative but more difficult and more valid logic can be avoided.

Discussion

Scapegoating is typically a short-term solution with short-term gains. It is executed in order to avoid more difficult realities. What is often seen in political or social environments can also be seen in business. The previous example may be extreme but there are many times when a common enemy maybe involved in order to avoid difficult realities. Think of the "new" economy, social change, government regulation, geopolitical forces, a turnover in technology, and so on. When your competition responds to these changes better than your company does who gets blamed? Do you scapegoat the change or do you find accountability in your own company not being able to respond to change as well as your competition has?

Dealing with Scapegoating

Scapegoating is about misplaced accountability. So the only way to deal with it is from an angle of accountability. Is the regulation, geopolitical forces, the technology, disintermediation, social change, and so on, to blame? Is this where accountability lies? Taking accountability is often hard for an organization to do when it's easier to blame some exogenous bogeyman. Every organization responds differently to accountability so it's hard to give specific advice on this topic. However, once the door to accountability has been cracked open there are some tools that can be used to further the discussion.

The use of SWOT analysis (Strengths, Weaknesses, Opportunities, and Threats) would help uncover internal versus external causes as well as understanding helpful or harmful responses.

Porter's Five Forces model would also be applicable and beneficial in some cases. Porter invented his model because he thought the SWOT analysis was overly simplistic and didn't meet the needs of a competitive business environment.

There are multiple versions of PEST analysis. P.E.S.T. stands for political, economic, social, and technological. Some people add more letters for things such as environmental or legal. Regardless of the mnemonic, this framework is used to be able to document the exogenous factors that should be considered—not scapegoated—in a good 4P's strategy.

"The search for a scapegoat is the easiest of all hunting expeditions," said President Dwight Eisenhower.

Selective Attention

Location: Customer experience and insights meeting.

Issue: Which features did customers like best for the new product we are working on?

Darwin (customer insights expert and consultant): *"This research was conducted in three rounds. The first round was used to get us pointed in the right direction with some qualitative interviews. In the second round, we did a large number of surveys to bring some quantitative information behind our thoughts. And, lastly, in the third round we followed up with some focus groups."*

Chekov (product development program manager): *"Yes, your work was brilliant. In all three rounds I see some verbatim comments that support our new Fetzer valve. I think this substantiates our product design work, and we need to continue the application process for a patent on that Fetzer valve."*

Scott (product line manager): *"I did see one or two positive comments. But I also think I saw a lot of positive comments about the good ol' Acme valve."*

Darwin: *"Yeah, Scott you are right. We had 23.8 times more favorable responses to the Acme valve."*

Chekov seems like he might be biased? Good thing Darwin is a professional.

Definition: *Selective Attention* comes right after selective hearing. Selective attention is using only a portion of a data set in an argument and discounting all the others. Usually this is done when the selected data fits an already presumed conclusion. A critical part of this definition is the fact that a small but erroneous data set is used in the face of a larger or more valid data set. If only erroneous data were available, then the failure would be due poor research methods, not selective attention.

Discussion

In this scenario, Chekov selects some verbatim results from the three rounds of customer insights work that fits his already presumed conclusion. He wants to continue the design work around his patent. This bias is giving him selective hearing and, as a result, his selective attention is drawn to the few results that support the conclusion he was hoping for.

Dealing with Selective Attention

Aside from the political, emotional, and other human factors involved with selective attention, dealing with this logical fallacy is fairly easy. Why? Because, by definition, you already have a larger set of data around which an alternative conclusion can and should be made.

So the solution is already on the table. A simple response of, *"Let's look at all the data and not just a portion,"* should get even the most biased meeting participants headed in the right direction. Other options are to ask:

- *"Is that the conclusion after using all of the data?"*
- *"If we analyzed all of the data, what is the conclusion?"* or
- *"If we were to set that data aside and analyze the rest, what would our conclusions be?"*

Slippery Slope

Location: In a car, driving to a veterinarian's office.

Issue: The regional sales manager and the account manager of a small-animal pharmaceutical manufacturer are discussing whether the company should offer point-of-sale (POS) materials to veterinarians for displaying the manufacturer's new line of flea collars.

Shelly (regional sales manager): *"What ideas do you have regarding how we might best promote our new flea collar?"*

David (account manager): *"I think we should give them a special display that they can put in their office that will prompt the customer to ask the vet about this new flea collar—our new flea collar."*

Shelly: *"Not sure that will work, David. We don't want these vets thinking we should supply them with POS materials every time we come out with a new product. We need to sell our products to vets on their merits. They are professionals, they'll do what's in the customers' best interest—they don't need POS stuff. If we give them that, they'll want us to give them other things, probably even want us to give them a discount too. Then we won't be making any money."*

Shelly is using the "slippery slope" fallacy to shoot down David's idea: Once you give veterinarians free POS materials, they'll want other "things" provided free, and the company's profits will evaporate.

Definition: The *Slippery Slope* argument presents a series of *weak* conditional claims. If you accept the first claim, then the last claim—which is undesirable—is presented as highly plausible to occur. The structure of a Slippery Slope argument looks like this:

A → B	If A, then B
B → C	If B, then C
C → D	If C, then D
not-D	D is undesirable
Therefore, not-A	Therefore, to avoid D, avoid A

Discussion

Politicians often use Slippery Slope fallacies to attack an opponent. *"If we do what my esteemed colleague across the aisle proposes, our country will quickly become a socialist state!"* But if you've been in business for at least a few years, you've likely heard someone use the Slippery Slope fallacy to criticize one of your or a fellow colleague's recommendations.

But the structure of this type of argument is not what makes it a fallacy. What makes it a fallacy is, when going from one premise to another, a "link" is not logically justified or empirically supported. In the aforementioned vignette, Shelly's slippery slope argument is structured as follows:

"If we give veterinarians free POS materials (A), then they will want more free stuff (B)."

"If we give them more free stuff (B), then they'll want us to give them discounts on our products (C)."

"If we give discounts on our products (C), then our profits will evaporate (D)."

Shelly complicates deciphering the goodness of her argument by making additional claims that are actually good claims:

"We need to sell our products to vets on their merits."

"They'll do what's in the customers' best interest."

Based on the authors' experiences in this industry, we can state that Shelly's argument is not plausible. *A* does not lead to *B*; *B* does not lead to *C*; although *C* can lead to *D*. Consequently, a Slippery Slope fallacy is only as strong as its weakest link. *C* may lead to *D*, but *A* does not lead to *D* because the other "links"—*A* to *B* and *B* to *C* are not plausible.

Keep in mind that some slippery slope arguments may not be fallacies! If the argument's premises are indeed plausible and logically linked to the conclusion, then this would be a good argument.

Dealing with Slippery Slope

The key to deciphering the strength of a slippery slope argument to discover if it is fallacious or not is to examine its premises—are they plausible—and the logical connection between the premises and the conclusion—is this logical connection strong? Some slippery slope arguments in marketing may be strong. For example:

"If our sales people are not given proper product education (A), they will be unable to explain the features and benefits of our product (B)."

"If they are unable to explain the features and benefits of our product (B), then our customers will not believe our product is priced competitively (C)."

"If our customers do not believe our product is priced competitively (C), our product sales, therefore, will suffer (D)."

These premises are all plausible and they are logically linked to the argument's conclusion (D).

One way to uncover whether a slippery slope argument is fallacious or not is to identify:

- To what extent each of the argument's premises is true or at least plausible? What evidence speaks to their plausibility?
- Which "link" in the argument is the weakest? Is it insufficiently strong enough to render the argument as a whole weak?

- Whether the premises are logically linked to the conclusion? In other words, if you accept the argument's premises, is the conclusion plausible?

Arguments with multiply linked premises can take you down a logically tortuous path. Don't slip.

Special Pleading

Location: Marketing conference room.

Issue: Product and marketing managers are reviewing the findings from the first phase of the organization's stage-gate process for new product development. (A *stage-gate* process is a systematic process for evaluating and measuring consumer reactions to new product ideas before a product is launched.)

> Mary (marketing research manager): *"As you know, the first step in our stage-gate process was to obtain consumer feedback on our new product idea in a series of focus groups we conducted in our top five markets. The results were quite positive, and I suggest we advance this product idea to Stage 2, where we develop a prototype product and conduct one-on-one interviews with prospective customers."*

> Jack (product manager): *"But Mary, I think you'll agree that the reaction we got in those focus groups was overwhelmingly positive—I think the most positive of all ideas that we've ever tested in our stage-gate process. There is pressure on us to come out with a new product by year's end. I recommend we skip the rest of the stage-gate process and go right to development. It will also give us a jump on our competition."*

Jack is using the "special pleading" fallacy to advance his case that the new product idea should not be subject to the organization's complete stage-gate process, which is against corporate policy.

Definition: *Special Pleading* is defined as "applying standards, principles, and/or rules to other people or circumstances, while making oneself or certain circumstances exempt from the same critical criteria, without providing adequate justification."[25]

Discussion

Special Pleading is often infused with emotion as opposed to reason, and it is often promulgated by associates who have an emotional investment in the outcome. In Jack's case, the "overwhelmingly positive" reaction by the focus group participants leads him to believe that the tested product idea will be a success, and the advantages of going to market as quickly as possible—for example, to meet an internal marketing goal and getting "a jump on the competition"—outweigh what little perceived risk there is of a marketing misfire.

Jack's reasons for wanting to skip ahead may be good ones: competition breathing down the company's back, obsolete products, and other unstated issues that make seeking a faster introduction beneficial or necessary. In our experience, however, processes such as stage-gate do protect against squandering resources on developing and marketing flawed products. However, these processes can have downsides, making what are clearly great ideas jump through unnecessary hoops and slowing time to market.

Jack's pleading, however, does not give good enough reasons for senior management to accept his argument. Organizations establish stage-gate processes to reduce needless levels of product development and marketing risk that come about by doing exactly what Jack suggests—skipping stages of a systematic examination of new product ideas prior to developing and launching new products. The criteria he wants to apply to this particular case differ from those that all other new product ideas in the organization are subject to.

Dealing with Special Pleading

If one of your associates accuses you of using Special Pleading to advance an argument, honestly examine their critique. Using the fallacy is tempting when an idea is yours, so examine the actual reasons you're giving to support your argument—are they good enough?

In Jack's situation, he might be able to make a good argument if he could show that "overwhelmingly positive" reactions to a product idea in the first step of their stage-gate process most nearly always turns out to be successful. But even in this situation, Jack has two strikes against him. First, "most nearly always" is not 100 percent, and the costs of a product failure might be damaging to the organization's long-run health and market position. Second, stage-gate processes accomplish more than just discovering whether an idea has market potential or not. In addition to providing justification for "go/no go" decisions, they also elicit valuable information on the marketing mix as well—for example, how the product should be priced and/or which advertising media and messages will optimize brand awareness and consideration.

However, even though we are making a special plea to you, our readers, to avoid using logical fallacies in your arguments, that does not mean that we should be held to the same standard when pleading to your colleagues to buy this book!

The General Rule

Location: Sales management planning meeting at a regional insurance company.

Issue: The company markets property and casualty insurance through independent insurance agencies. The team regularly convenes in December to plan the next year's agency sales calls.

> Jim (marketing VP): *"This year, we have 150 agencies to visit in person—20 more than last year—and we like to arrange these meetings during the first four months of the year. As a rule of thumb, the meetings last about 60 minutes, so each of the management teams can schedule three to four meetings a day."*

> Brian (sales manager): *"I'm wondering whether we should vary the times we spend with each agency and maybe visit some agencies two or three times during the year instead of just once. I know our company is growing and, in the past, this rule of thumb seems to have worked; but our new market segmentation strategy suggests that we need to spend more time with some agencies over others."*

> Jim: *"As you said, our company is growing." This rule of thumb has served us well in the past, and there is certainly no evidence that it isn't working*

now. Let's just keep it simple—it will make all this scheduling easier, and we have a lot to do this year."

General rules of thumb do simplify the hectic schedules of us marketers, and we should not necessarily give them up. But sometimes these rules are simply not good reasons to justify routine procedures established over time.

Definition: *The General Rule*, also known as the "accident" fallacy, presumes that there are no good exceptions to a general rule, when in fact there are.

Discussion

Admittedly, we need to use general rules just to make it through the day safely—be aware of oncoming traffic when approaching a "yield" sign, don't gulp down hot coffee, be careful when handling a sharp knife. These general rules often apply in conducting many business functions as well. For example, financial auditing practices or quality control procedures often dictate specific, unwavering protocols. They are based on historical experience showing that, if they are not followed, fiduciary responsibility and product quality can be compromised. In short, there are good reasons not to stray from some general rules.

In marketing, however, the wise words of Oxford University scholar Robert Burton (1577–1640) often apply, "No rule is so general, which admits not some exception." One is guilty of using the General Rule fallacy when applying an accepted rule—"That's the procedure we've always followed"—to a specific case (or cases) without relevant grounds for doing so, as in the earlier example. Motivated by convenience and efficiency, Jim applies a past rule of thumb for scheduling agency meetings indiscriminately, when a market segmentation study suggests that different segments of agencies should be treated differently, vis-à-vis the frequency and length of sales calls. Moreover, when claims that "there is certainly no evidence that [this general rule] isn't working," he provides no evidence that he is making a good decision.

Dealing with the General Rule

This can be a particularly vexing fallacy to deal with, especially if it comes from a boss or colleague who has a frantic schedule with very little time to catch her breath. Here are some suggestions:

- Give examples of exceptions made to other general rules that worked out well. Brian might have said, *"In our customer call center, we have lots of rules and procedures. But do you recall that policy you implemented a couple years ago that gave the customer service rep discretion to give complete refunds on purchases of less than $200, instead of getting permission from the call center supervisor, which typically took two to three days? You felt that this kind of flexibility would improve customer loyalty. And it did!"*
- Show how an exception to a rule helps further a more strategic organizational objective. Consider the following response: *"I agree that we all need to manage our time efficiently. But in the larger picture, our company has embraced a new market segmentation strategy, which holds significant promise to increase our sales and profits."*
- If possible, show that the exception has no significant resource implications. For instance, spending more time with some agencies and less time with others may have the same end result in costs and employee time as if the general rule were followed.

In marketing, it's a general rule that general rules have exceptions.

The Ludic Fallacy

Location: Pharmaceutical marketing "war room."

Issue: Planning the advertising rollout of an over-the-counter flu remedy prior to the fall flu season.

Kevin (senior big data analyst): *"In one of our recent Big Data projects, we examined tracking the word "flu" in Google's search engine and found a high correlation between people doing Google searches on the word "flu" and retail sales."*

Laura (VP sales): *"Wow, Kevin, that's an amazing result. Think about how we can use that information to manage inventory at the regional level, as well as to fine-tune our Internet ads and POS."*

Raechel (logistics analyst): *"That's a great idea. Our team can work with Kevin's and develop an inventory and distribution strategy for the next flu season."*

Laura: *"And I'll schedule a meeting with our digital group to work with them on fine-tuning our digital strategy."*

This invented and abridged conversation certainly seems plausible, given that it is partly true. Google did publish an article in one of the top scientific journals, *Nature,* describing how accurately "Google Flu Trends" tracked the spread of that virus in 2008.[26] So, about now you might be asking, "Where is the fallacy here?" It emerges when we look at what happened a year after those data were analyzed, when the U.S. flu season seems to have confounded Google's algorithms.

Definition: Google fell victim to the *Ludic Fallacy*, in which highly precise (notice, we say "precise" not "accurate") statistical and probabilistic models fail to model the nuances of the real world. Google's estimate for the number of cases during the 2009 Christmas peak of national flu season was almost double that of the Centers for Disease Control (CDC), and some of its state data showed even larger discrepancies.

Discussion

"Ludic" comes from the Latin word "game," and was popularized by Nassim Nicholas Taleb in his 2007 book, *The Black Swan.* In his book, Taleb contends that complex statistical models and algorithms—the outputs of which are often used to support marketing arguments—are inherently biased because of the following factors:

- All relevant information about a topic is not in the possession of the statistician or the decision maker;
- Small changes in the premises supporting a forecast may have large implications in the forecast; and,
- These models cannot take into account events that have never happened—for example, the mortgage crisis of 2008.

These factors are especially relevant to marketers who rely on marketing research that incorporates statistical analyses—especially in regard to modeling consumers' anticipated purchasing behavior. With respect to these studies, you should realize the following:

- Researchers cannot measure all facets of all consumer beliefs that affect brand choice. Human belief systems are simply too complex. *"Not everything that counts can be counted"* is a quote often attributed to Albert Einstein, but most likely originated from a book written by William Bruce Cameron.[27]
- There are many factors surrounding consumer behavior that are impossible to measure, for example, how one's competitors' will respond to a marketing effort.
- What is measured in marketing research studies is not measured without error. For example, survey respondents are notorious for their poor top of mind recall in reporting past brand-purchasing behaviors.

And, to underscore the major weaknesses of highly precise statistical models is Taleb's Black Swan—the unforeseeable event (i.e., it was once believed that all swans were white, until a black swan—an unforeseeable event—was discovered in Australia).

Dealing with the Ludic Fallacy

How does one, then, ensure that the Ludic Fallacy does not infect one's marketing arguments? We have several suggestions:

- First, all marketing research findings need to be combined with management's background knowledge. Ask the question, *"Are the research findings logically consistent with everything we know about this subject matter?"* If not, investigate. *"Don't let the numbers do the thinking for you."*

- Second, brainstorm alternative scenarios regarding a marketing effort, based on different assumptions. For example, when launching a new product, consider different launch scenarios based on different competitive responses or changes to the economy. The goal is not necessarily to uncover these Black Swans as it is to be flexible and adaptive as you determine that not all of the assumptions on which the launch plan is built are actually correct.

- Third, as we've discussed in previous vignettes, don't confuse *correlation* with *causation* in any Big Data or marketing research analysis. If you're not sure or misinterpret what is causing the correlation between two factors, then you don't really understand what can derail that correlation.

Regarding the last point, in examining customer satisfaction scores and sales for a major power sports manufacturer, management discovered a positive correlation between sales and customer satisfaction, which management attributed *solely* to their product's quality. Over time, as the company grew, these satisfaction scores declined although product quality—as measured by metrics such as warranty claims—stayed constant. The problem was that, as the company got larger and took on more independent distributors, the quality of the distributors' customer service declined. This was not discovered until some damage had been done to their brand equity. Had managers better understood what was causing the initial high customer satisfaction scores, they could have been more proactive in screening and managing the independent dealer network.

Don't let the numbers do your thinking.

Strawman

Note to reader: The Strawman and Red Herring fallacies are often confused, so we discuss both in this vignette.

Location: Corporate vehicle driving north of Ankeny, Iowa, on Interstate 35 toward Minneapolis. Occupants are the VP of marketing and the regional sales rep for the company's Minnesota region. They work for a firm that sells machine tools to heavy equipment manufacturers.

Issue: The two are discussing future pricing strategy.

> Henry (regional sales rep): *"The sales planning committee's consensus is that we should continue our discount program for orders over $500,000 and then give customers price breaks on every $250,000 over that amount. We need to do this to stay competitive in the marketplace and encourage our customers to give us larger orders. This might be a good time to give me your feedback since we are alone and you can speak more candidly."*

> Elizabeth (vice president of marketing): *"Well, as you know, I've always been against giving price discounts; it cheapens our product. Most of the committee members are in the sales department, and all they want to do is make their job easier. So I'm against it. Anyway, the real barrier to increasing sales is not price; it's our follow-up service department. If they would do a better job servicing our clients after the sale, clients would be beating a path to our door."*

Elizabeth is lobbing two logical fallacies at Henry. Her first volley is the "strawman," followed quickly on its heels by the "red herring."

Definition: The *Strawman* fallacy occurs when a person distorts or misinterprets the original argument because it is easier to criticize the inaccurate version than the original one. The *Red Herring* fallacy occurs when a person, after being confronted with an argument, simply changes the topic to some other issue not related to the original discussion.

Discussion

By using the Strawman fallacy, Elizabeth distorts Henry's argument for the pricing strategy when she says that, *"Most of the committee members are in the sales department, and all they want to do is make their job easier."* That may be true, but Elizabeth is mischaracterizing Henry's premise for the price discount program, which states that the rationale for doing so is to be price-competitive and encourage customers to place larger orders. If Elizabeth wants to refute Henry's argument, she needs to give good reasons why his claims are false and not malign the motivation of other committee members. For example, Elizabeth might identify competitors who don't offer price discounts but, nevertheless, are able to generate large orders because of some other factor, such as excellent service after the sale.

In trying to make her criticism even stronger, Elizabeth follows up with the following Red Herring fallacy: *"Anyway, the real barrier to increasing sales is not price; it's our service department. If they would do a better job servicing our clients after the sale, clients would be beating a path to our door."* Her strategy here is to focus on a different argument and, by winning that argument, Elizabeth believes she also, in effect, wins the initial argument.

As we talked about in a separate discussion of the Red Herring fallacy, its history is noteworthy: One of the ways fox hunters in England would train their dogs to stay on the trail of the fox was to drag smelly fish—for example, red herrings—across the fox's trail before unleashing the dogs. The idea was to train the dogs to ignore the fish scent and continue after the fox. Keep this image in mind the next time you want to accurately diagnose whether the Strawman versus the Red Herring fallacy is being used. The latter changes the argument's subject; the former simply misrepresents or distorts the original argument.

Dealing with Strawman and Red Herring

Since you are not likely to use either of these fallacies in your conversations with associates, we discuss how you should respond if someone tosses a strawman or red herring your way.

When these fallacies are used, they are often unreflective, quick retorts to an argument you've offered. Don't embarrass the person by showing him how illogical he is—especially in a group setting. Rather, consider the following strategies:

- In reacting to a Strawman fallacy, simply explain that the person's interpretation of your argument is not what you intended to say. For example, Henry could have sought to diffuse Elizabeth's criticism by saying something like: *"I did not explain myself well, Elizabeth. Let me elaborate on why*

*I think being both price competitive and offering customers
an incentive to buy more product are good reasons for a price
discount strategy."* Then, Henry can strengthen his argument by citing good evidence supporting his claim, thereby
directing the conversation back to an accurate interpretation
of what he is arguing for.

- In reacting to a Red Herring fallacy, acknowledge that the
  person's criticism may be legitimate, but that it is a different
  subject than what you were addressing in your argument. For
  example, Henry might have said the following, *"The service
  department issue that you raise is a good point, and let's discuss
  that after we have resolved my initial argument supporting a
  price discount strategy."*

Get your critics to focus on the actual premises and conclusions of
your arguments, rather than misinterpretations and irrelevant side topics.
Choking on strawmen and red herrings makes it difficult to articulate
your claims and recommendations clearly and accurately.

Notes

Chapter 1

1. Burkitt and Bruno (2010).
2. Harvard Business Review (n.d.).
3. Baldoni (2010).
4. Taylor (2010, 1).
5. Engler (2013).
6. Green (2012).
7. Glaser (1941, 52).
8. LeBlanc (1998, 2).
9. Internet Encyclopedia of Philosophy (n.d.).
10. Doyle (2010).
11. Bennett (2012, 7).
12. Sharp (2010, 171–76).
13. deLaplante (2014).

Chapter 2

1. DeLaplante (2016).
2. Internet Encyclopedia of Philosophy (n.d.).
3. Internet Encyclopedia of Philosophy (n.d.).
4. One factor that helps you decide whether an argument is deductive or inductive is the intention of the person making the argument—does she intend her argument to be deductive, that is, iron-clad plausible if the premises are iron-clad true/plausible; or inductive, where the conclusion is at best plausible? See "Deductive Arguments and Valid Reasoning" at http://criticalthinkeracademy.com/courses/argument-ninja/lectures/51532
5. Fishken (2008).

Chapter 4

1. Sharp (2010), 488.
2. Curtis (n.d.).
3. Curtis (n.d.).
4. Bryant (2013).

Chapter 5

1. Angst (n.d.).
2. Hamm (n.d.).
3. *Wikipedia* (n.d.), retrieved from http: en.wikipedia.org/wiki/Boo.com
4. Surowiecki (2005).
5. Rogers (1995).
6. Sharp (2010), Chapter 2.
7. Private correspondence between Byron Sharp and Terry Grapentine. Sharp also discusses this topic on pages 112-113 of his textbook (2013), *Marketing: Theory, Evidence, Practice.*
8. Zelm (2014).
9. *Wikipedia* (n.d). Retrieved from en.wikipedia.org/wiki/Moon_landing_conspiracy_theories
10. The Telegraph (2009).
11. Bouty (2015).
12. Jenson (2005).
13. *Wikipedia* (n.d.). Retrieved from: en.wikipedia.org/wiki/Ropes_course
14. Sharp (2013, 249).
15. Blitz Team (2015).
16. *Wikipedia* (n.d.). Retrieved from en.wikipedia.org/wiki/List_of_cognitive_biases
17. Wikiquote (n.d.). Retrieved from en.wikiquote.org/wiki/Helmuth_von_Moltke_the_Elder
18. Agilemethodology (n.d.)
19. Brainyquote (n.d.).
20. Forbes (n.d.).
21. deLaplante (2016), Section 9.
22. Highouse (2015).
23. Highouse (2015).
24. Schall and Smith (2000).
25. Bennett (2012, 201).
26. Ginsberg et al. (2009).
27. O'Toole (2010).

References

Agilemethodology. n.d. "The Agile Movement." Retrieved from http://agilemethodology.org/

Amster-Burton, M. 2010. "Price Anchoring, or Why a $499 iPad Seems Inexpensive." Retrieved from https://blog.mint.com/how-to/price-anchoring/

Angst, T. n.d. "Logical Fallacies by Todangst." Retrieved from http://freethoughtpedia.com/wiki/Logical_Fallacies_by_Todangst#Ad_Fidentia

Baldoni, J. January 20, 2010. *How Leaders Should Think Critically.* Cambridge, MA: Harvard Business Review. Retrieved from //blogs.hbr.org/2010/01/how-leaders-should-think-criti/

Bennett, B. 2012. *Logically … Fallacious: The Ultimate Collection of Over 300 Logical Fallacies.* Sudbury, MA: eBookit.com.

Blitz Team. 2015. "Things More Likely to Kill You Than a Plane Crash." Retrieved from http://blitz.arc.unsw.edu.au/2015/things-more-likely-to-kill-you-than-a-plane-crash/

Bouty, L. 2015. "Marketing Failure Case: Colgate Kitchen Entrees." Retrieved from www.bouty.net/blog/2015/07/marketing-failure-case-colgate-kitchen-entrees/

Brainyquote. n.d. "Carl von Clausewitz Quotes." Retrieved from www.brainyquote.com/quotes/quotes/c/carlvoncla399732.html

Bryant, A. 2013. "In Head Hunting, Big Data May Not Be Such a Big Deal." *The New York Times.* Retrieved from www.nytimes.com/2013/06/20/business/in-head-hunting-big-data-may-not-be-such-a-big-deal.html?pagewanted=2&_r=0

Burkitt, L., and K. Bruno. 2010. "New, Improved, and Failed." *Forbes.com on NBC News.com.* Retrieved from www.nbcnews.com/id/36005036/ns/business-forbes_com/t/new-improved-failed/#.V1Xww_krLIU

Curtis, G.N. n.d. "Bad Reasons Fallacy." Fallacy Files. Retrieved from www.fallacyfiles.org/badreasn.html

deLaplante, K. 2014. "The Five Pillars of Critical Thinking." Retrieved from http://criticalthinkeracademy.com/courses/what-is-critical-thinking/lectures/51621

deLaplante, K. 2016. "Critical Thinking Academy: Learn to Think Like a Philosopher." Retrieved from www.udemy.com/critical-thinker-academy/#%2F

Doyle, J. May 10, 2010. "Apple, Rising: 1976–1985." *PopHistoryDig.com.* Retrieved from www.pophistorydig.com/topics/tag/apple-vs-ibm/

Engler, J. May 14, 2013. "Necessary to Compete." Business Roundtable. Retrieved from http://businessroundtable.org/media/news-releases/necessary-to-compete

Fishken, R. 2008. "10 Irrational Human Behaviors and How to Leverage Them to Improve Web Marketing." Retrieved from https://moz.com/blog/10-irrational-human-behaviors-how-to-leverage-them-to-improve-web-marketing

Forbes. n.d. "Most Annoying Business Jargon." Retrieved from www.forbes.com/pictures/ekij45gdh/most-annoying-business-jargon/

Ginsberg, J., M.H. Mohebbi, R.S. Patel, L. Brammer, M.S. Smolinski and L. Brilliant. 2009. "Detecting Influenza Epidemics Using Search Engine Query Sata." Nature. Retrieved from www.nature.com/nature/journal/v457/n7232/full/nature07634.html

Glaser, E. 1941. *An Experiment in the Development of Critical Thinking.* New York: Teacher's. www.criticalthinking.org/pages/defining-critical-thinking/766

Green, H. 2012. "How to develop 5 Critical Thinking Types." *Forbes*, March 17. Retrieved from www.forbes.com/sites/work-in-progress/2012/03/27/how-to-develop-5-critical-thinking-types/#186f85157838

Hamm, M. n.d. "Mia Hamm Quotes." Retrieved from www.goodreads.com/quotes/120121-many-people-say-i-m-the-best-women-s-soccer-player-in

Harvard Business Review. n.d. "Case Study." Retrieved from https://hbr.org/store/case-studies?cm_mmc=cpc-_-google-_-domestic-_-cases&referral=02276&utm_source=google&utm_medium=cpc&utm_campaign=dom_cases&gclid=CjwKEAjwn7e8BRCUqZiP_vnrtBkSJAC_lp4HPhw99fdb8uGGCxHuhNQb40EIga0aCoBDvTcJcg2K3RoCruDw_wcB

Internet Encyclopedia of Philosophy. n.d. "Fallacies." Retrieved from www.iep.utm.edu/fallacy/

Jenson, N. 2005. "Counterfactuals." Retrieved from http://onegoodmove.org/1gm/1gmarchive/2005/03/counterfactuals.html

Kahneman, D. 2011. *Thinking Fast, and Slow.* New York: Farrar, Straus and Giroux.

LeBlanc, J. 1998. *Thinking Clearly: A Guide to Critical Reasoning.* New York: W.W. Norton & Company.

O'Toole, G. 2010. "Not Everything that Counts Can Be Counted." The Quote Investigator. Retrieved from quoteinvestigator.com/2010/05/26/everything-counts-einstein/

Rogers, E.M. 1995. *Diffusion of Innovations.* 5th ed. New York: Free Press.

Schall, E.M., and G. Smith. 2000. "Do Baseball Players Regress Toward the Mean?" *The American Statistician* 54, no. 4, pp. 231–35.

Sharp, B. 2010. *How Brands Grow: What Marketers Don't Know.* Victoria, Australia: Oxford University Press.

Sharp, B. 2013. *Marketing: Theory, Evidence, Practice.* Victoria, Australia: Oxford.

Surowiecki, J. 2005. *The Wisdom of Crowds.* New York. Anchor Books.

Taylor, M. 2010. "Schools, Businesses Focus on Critical Thinking." *The Wall Street Journal Online*, September 12. Retrieved from www.wsj.com/articles/ SB10001424052748703882304575466100773788806

The Phrase Finder. n.d. "The Meaning and Origin of the Expression: A Stitch in Time Saves Nine." Retrieved from www.phrases.org.uk/meanings/a-stitch-in-time.html

The Telegraph. 2009. "Apollo 11 Hoax: One in Four People Do Not Believe in Moon Landing." Retrieved from www.telegraph.co.uk/news/science/ space/5851435/Apollo-11-hoax-one-in-four-people-do-not-believe-in-moon-landing.html

Wikipedia. n.d. "Boo.com." Retrieved from https://en.wikipedia.org/wiki/Boo. com

Wikipedia. n.d. "List of Cognitive Biases." Retrieved from https://en.wikipedia. org/wiki/List_of_cognitive_biases

Wikipedia. n.d. "Moon Landing Conspiracy Theories." Retrieved from https:// en.wikipedia.org/wiki/Moon_landing_conspiracy_theories

Wikipedia. n.d. "Ropes Course." Retrieved from https://en.wikipedia.org/wiki/ Ropes_course

Wikiquote. n.d. "Helmuth von Moltke the Elder." Retrieved from https:// en.wikiquote.org/wiki/Helmuth_von_Moltke_the_Elder

Zelm, A. 2014. "Are These 4 Marketing Fads Dragging Your Strategy Down?" Retrieved from www.kunocreative.com/blog/bid/89613/Are-These-4-Marketing-Fads-Dragging-Your-Strategy-Down

Index

OTHER TITLES IN OUR MARKETING STRATEGY COLLECTION

Naresh Malhotra, Georgia Tech, Editor

- *Sales Promotion Decision Making: Concepts, Principles, and Practice* by Steve Ogden-Barnes and Stella Minahan
- *Smart Marketing: How to Dramatically Grow Your Revenue* by Ahmed Al Akber
- *Market Sensing Today* by Melvin Prince and Constantinos-Vasilios Priporas
- *Launching New Products: Best Marketing and Sales Practices* by John Westman and Paul Sowyrda
- *Marketing Plan Templates for Enhancing Profits* by Elizabeth Rush Kruger
- *Relationship Marketing Re-Imagined: Marketing's Inevitable Shift from Exchanges to Value Cocreating Relationships* by Naresh K. Malhotra, Can Uslay, and Ahmet Bayraktar
- *Service Excellence: Creating Customer Experiences that Build Relationships* by Ruth N. Bolton
- *Critical Thinking for Marketers: Learn How to Think, Not What to Think, Volume II* by David Dwight, Terry Grapentine, and David Soorholtz

Announcing the Business Expert Press Digital Library

Concise e-books business students need for classroom and research

This book can also be purchased in an e-book collection by your library as

- a one-time purchase,
- that is owned forever,
- allows for simultaneous readers,
- has no restrictions on printing, and
- can be downloaded as PDFs from within the library community.

Our digital library collections are a great solution to beat the rising cost of textbooks. E-books can be loaded into their course management systems or onto students' e-book readers.
The **Business Expert Press** digital libraries are very affordable, with no obligation to buy in future years. For more information, please visit **www.businessexpertpress.com/librarians**. To set up a trial in the United States, please email **sales@businessexpertpress.com**.

CPSIA information can be obtained
at www.ICGtesting.com
Printed in the USA
LVOW04s1008230117
521852LV00015B/566/P